And Time
Stood Still

Alice Taylor

I was born on a hillside farm in North Cork near the Kerry border overlooking an inspirational view from the McGillycuddy Reeks to the Galtee Mountains; it was akin to looking out at a giant watercolour painting. This farm and amazing landscape were the inspiration for my first six books and maybe, in many ways, for all my books. When I married a wonderful man I came to live in the little village of Innishannon in West Cork, and have been here ever since. Innishannon continued the inspiration begun on the home farm. It was a busy life, running the village shop, post office and a guest house, and rearing children, as well as being involved in all village activity. I love this village and have written about it in *The Village* and *The Parish*. For many years I was part of a busy, crowded household. I love gardening, painting and writing, and have two lively black Doberman dogs who keep me company.

ALICE'S BOOKS:
To School through the Fields
Quench the Lamp
The Night before Christmas
A Country Miscellany
Country Days
The Village
The Parish
The Journey
The Woman of the House
Across the River
House of Memories
An Evening with Alice Taylor (tape)

And Time Stood Still

Alice Taylor

BRANDON

First published 2012 by
Brandon
an imprint of The O'Brien Press
12 Terenure Road East, Rathgar,
Dublin 6, Ireland.

Tel: +353 1 4923333; Fax: +353 1 4922777
E-mail: books@obrien.ie.
Website: www.obrien.ie

ISBN: 978-1-84717-332-4

Photographs, including cover image: Emma Byrne;
with thanks to Laura Feeney for plough p6; Mogue Doyle for collar and
hames p45 and harness bridle p120; Mogue and Brigid Byrne for seat p37.

British Library Cataloguing-in-Publication Data
A catalogue record for this title
is available from the British Library

1 2 3 4 5 6 7 8
12 13 14 15 16

Printed and bound in the Czech Republic
by Finidr
The paper used in this book is produced
using pulp from managed forests

Dedication

For those who brought love and joy to my life
and to you now walking the memory road.

Contents

Preface

Nothing prepares us for the ferocity of grief. The death of those we love disturbs our deepest roots and catapults us – bruised, broken and unprepared – on to the path of grief. Time seems to stand still. Even the word 'death' strikes a chill in the mind. Mostly we ignore it and avoid using it, like people walking backwards towards a cliff edge. But no matter what we call it, when a loved one goes over that edge we are whipped around and made to look death straight in the face. Then the hurting encompasses us like a shroud; pain takes hold and clings us to that black space.

Someone who was part of your world is gone and has taken a chunk of you with them. As well as taking your loved one, death has also taken part of you. A beloved limb has been amputated and you are left with a raw, bleeding wound. Grief is physical as well as mental. You cannot eat and you cannot sleep. Your energy has evaporated and your coping skills have shrunk. Small decisions have turned into major challenges and your threshold of tolerance had disintegrated.

You feel alone on this journey and nothing prepares you for its devastation. You walk around looking normal, but inside you are bleeding. The world has shrunk into a painful path and you seem to go round and round in circles. You are in a prison of desolation without walls.

The bewildering thing is that your loved one is still part of your everyday thinking and their presence is still all around you. Impossible as it seems, you are living in two worlds – the 'before' and the 'after'. These two worlds are not welded together, so your thinking is split and the ground beneath your feet is a deep chasm.

Reason and grief have no relationship. Grief is raw emotion; reason does not come into it. When someone you love dies, deep dormant feelings escape out of a previously unquarried reservoir – a roaring tide is let loose and it breaks down all barriers and sweeps on, creating mental chaos.

Waking up in the morning is the toughest part of the day. For one second before realisation dawns, the nightmare is not there. But then reality crashes in. There is no getting away from it: another day to get through!

You look around at people who have survived terrible trauma and wonder: How can they keep going? When I asked this of a friend, she replied sadly: 'There's no choice. If people didn't recover from grief the world would come to a standstill.' But in grief your world *is* at a standstill.

It is a time when prayer should help; but that may not be so. Your loved one has gone across the great divide where all your prayers have gone. Heaven is silent now and God may have become the God of no explanations.

In times of heartache I often turn to nature. In the dark of night when a fierce storm rages, the deep roots of a tree hold it in the earth, and similarly when we are battling through the storm of death and grief the human spirit can find within itself the power of amazing endurance. As we struggle on, tiny stepping-stones appear. They are created by kindness, nature and our own inner creative resources, and by a source above and beyond our human understanding.

Tears will help to soften the frozen lump of grief that has parked itself where your heart was and eventually a tiny bud of peace may tentatively begin to flower and fragile shoots of hope come and go. Time moves again, slowly at first. An Eastern sage said: 'Hope is like a road in the country where there wasn't ever a road – but when many people walk on it, the road comes into existence.'

Through the Eyes of a Child

Chapter 1

Little Brother

'What did you buy at the auction?' I enquired eagerly. 'An antique bed,' my sister told me. 'It's in the back room. Go and have a look.'

Full of anticipation, I walked hurriedly back the corridor, anxious to see her purchase, but when I opened the bedroom door I stood transfixed. The smell of sulphur permeated the room. At some point in its journey, her antique bed had absorbed the smell of a sulphur candle that now filled the air and curled up my nostrils. A chilling fibre of memory stirred in the deep recesses of my mind. Gradually other fibres awoke and wove themselves into a shroud that wrapped itself around me and dragged me back. Back through a whole lifetime.

I was six years of age, standing uncertainly outside the white bedroom door in the shadowy upstairs landing of our old farmhouse. A slim pencil of light from the narrow skylight overhead shone on the battered brass knob. I wanted to turn that dented knob and open the door, but dreaded doing so. One part of my mind knew that he would not be inside in the wooden bed, curled up in a little ball, breathing quietly. And yet he might be! As long as I didn't open the door there was always the hope, the possibility that it had all never happened. That I had imagined it. That it was not true. But once I opened that door I would know, know for sure that he was gone and would never again come back.

I finally turned the rattling brass knob and the door squeaked in protest. I edged it open just a few inches and peeped in through the narrow opening. The room was in shadow. A navy-blue blind was pulled down over the one small window. The big old wooden bed took up most of the room, the horsehair mattress and feather tick rolled up on its wire base. All sheets and blankets, signs of our sleeping comfort, were gone, whipped off and washed in tubs of disinfectant and hung for days on the clothes line in the grove behind the house.

In a white sconce on a small wicker table in front of the window stood a yellow sulphur candle. Its flame, edged with grey smoke, guttered and spluttered in a pool of hot candle grease that overflowed in little yellow streams down along its sides. Its heavy, cloying, acrid smell snaked upwards along the latticed walls, across the low, timber ceiling, around the edge of the door and curled up my nostrils. There was only one reason for that sulphur candle in the bedroom that we had shared since he had left the iron cot in our parents' bedroom: the sulphur candle was there to fumigate the room after his death. That smell told me that he was gone. He was gone and all that was left was this terrible smell.

The smell had a hypnotic effect on me. It terrified and repelled me, but in some horrific way it fascinated me too. Every day I peeped in and every day the smell of the sulphur candle told me the same story. It crept up my nose and into my memory box. It was the smell of his going. On that day in my sister's bedroom the smell of the sulphur candle melted the seal over my childhood trauma and the dead memory strands awoke. They catapulted me back in time.

In my earliest memory I am sitting on a warm flagstone on the doorstep of our old home while Connie sits in his pram under a huge palm tree in the garden. That old palm tree dominated our garden and its branches brushed against the window panes, filling the rooms at the far end of the house with moving shadows.

Connie and I were the youngest in a family of seven, so when the others were gone to school we were left to our own devices. The farmyard was our playground. We fed the baby ducks and goslings, but always with a wary eye on the gander, who did not like us. Feeding the hens was great excitement as flocks of birds swooped down to share the hens' breakfast. Later in the day it was our job to check the henhouse for fresh eggs and notify my mother that it was time for collection. Afterwards, Lady, the mother greyhound, could be let loose; she had an appetite for fresh eggs and had to be tied up until after egg collection – the other dogs and the cats posed no such problem so were free to roam around the yard and farm buildings. It was our job too to feed the cats at milking time from the rusty cover of an old churn. We also helped with the feeding of the calves but stood well back when they dived into the buckets of milk, as they could suddenly thrust the bucket forward in a fit of exuberance and injure unwisely positioned feet.

We had a pet calf, Richie, whom we singled out for special attention. He was a small, frail little fellow and we felt an affinity with him as he fought for his rights in the bigger herd. There was also a baby lamb whom we christened Sam. Sam had not made the grade out in the fields so he was reared in a butter-box by the fire, where he thrived so well on a bottle that he soon outgrew his limited accommodation and my father told us that he would have to be reunited with the others. Connie and I objected as feeding Sam with a bottle and teat while he was small and dainty was great fun. But one morning when he whipped the entire teat off the bottle, creating a waterfall of milk, we finally accepted that it was, indeed, time for him to move out to open spaces.

We often visited Bill, who lived at the top of the hill behind our house. We would climb up the steep slope between the tall ferns, resting along the way on the little flat stone seats that Bill had created for himself and where he would pause and rest as he drew water up from the well at the foot of the hill. When we reached the top we always sat by the scratching pole that my father had placed there for the cows. Bill would be waiting for us beyond the next ditch.

My father was always busy working his farm but Bill, even though he too had a farm, always seemed to have plenty of time to play with us. He gave us rides on his donkey and told us stories. We loved Bill. We would ramble home after our visit and meander into other fields and be missing for hours – and the only danger was the gander and neighbouring bulls.

But one disappearance did create panic. It was a very wet winter's morning and Connie went missing. The stream at the end of the yard had turned into an angry torrent that backed up into the front garden and also flooded the garden behind the house. Connie was nowhere to be found and the terror was that he had fallen into the flood waters. A thorough search proved that this was unlikely, but the possibility could not be ruled out. Every corner of the house and yards was searched, to no avail. Then I decided to visit our sheepdog who had had a litter of cuddly pups the previous week in the haybarn. And there, curled up with the new mother, was Connie, sound asleep, and almost indistinguishable from the pups draped all around him. On another occasion, Connie's ability to lie down and go to sleep whenever and wherever he got tired nearly gave my father a heart attack. Dad was out cutting the corn with the mowing machine, drawn by our two horses, Jerry and Paddy. Suddenly the horses came to a standstill and snorted in fright. My father came off the mowing machine to investigate the problem and found Connie sound asleep in the corn. If the horses had not alerted him to Connie's presence the consequences would have been horrific.

In the summer we played in the grove behind the house where we created other worlds. We played imaginary games beneath trees where the ground was soft with the fallen leaves and pine needles of many years. One old tree had a huge hole in its trunk. This was our treehouse and here we sat, pretending that we were travelling to many strange places. Because we could not see the top of the tree, it just seemed to go up and up, and we believed it grew up into heaven. Heaven, in those days, was very real and up there was God and the angels – and our cat who had died the year before. Everything that left our world finished up in heaven and we never questioned that. It was a happy place where one day we would all end up. Why would anyone not want to go there?

At night Connie and I slept together in a big bed that had a high, old-fashioned timber base and headboard. The fluffy tick, filled with soft duck-down collected over the years from the Christmas plucking, provided warmth – and fun too as we stood on the timber headboard and dived into its comforting fullness. In it we made sunken pathways and tunnels and it had countless hidden possibilities. Going to bed early, when sleep was the least of our interests, we turned the big bed into a playground peopled by imaginary friends and animals, and we scratched pictures on the headboard, and my mother never cautioned about damaging the paint-work. There were no dolls and teddies to cuddle in bed at the time as these were the war years and such luxuries were non-existent. But there was no shortage of statues in Irish homes, so instead our resourceful mother provided us with two little statues, one of St Theresa and the other of Baby Jesus. So every night we took our battered and much-loved statues to bed.

On Christmas morning when I was six, I awoke, moved my feet and something clanked against the bottom of the bed. It was a doll, with a hard China-ware face, and we chris-tened her Katie Maria. She was my first doll, and Connie got a little cloth man-doll that we called Patsy. We had many hours of fun with our two new friends, Katie Maria and Patsy, but did not abandon our two old pals who stood guard on our bedside table.

When summer came around again we returned to the grove and our treehouse. We lived in a child's wonderland and the harsh face of reality had not yet frowned on us. But then, suddenly, an icy draught blew around us when Connie got very sick. He had been part of my every day and night, sharing every childish secret, and now he could laugh no more. He lay still and quiet like a little bird in the middle of the feather bed. I sat on the floor and played endlessly with Katie Maria and Patsy. I wanted Connie to talk to me, but Connie was like the two statues and could not talk anymore. I whispered to him, feeling that even though he could not answer he might somehow still know that I was there. My mother would come and coax me out of the room and I got the feeling that in some way I should not be in there. But as soon as her back was turned I crept back in and sometimes hid under the bed. The doctor came every day to examine Connie and one day, from under the bed, I watched him and my mother silhouetted against the window as they discussed my little brother. My mother's face was no longer calm and serene. She did not look like herself anymore. When the doctor was gone she told me that Connie would have to go to hospital to get better, but looking into my mother's stricken face I sensed that he might never come back. Since he had got sick, my world had been filled with an unknown dread that something terrible was going to happen. Now the certainty formed a hard lump of terror inside me. I went up into the grove and sat into our treehouse.

Later that day a black car came into the yard and through the trees I watched my mother come out with Connie in her arms. He was wrapped in a white blanket, but my mother's face was whiter still.

I stayed in the grove all day, feeling close to Connie there. Tears never came. Crying was something you did when you cut your finger – this was beyond all tears. Finally, as dusk came, I heard the pine needles crush as someone approached. It was Bill. He sat outside the treehouse as he could not fit inside, sat saying nothing while tears ran down his face. I crept out of the tree and onto his lap, putting my arms around his neck. And so we sat, Bill and I, locked together in our terrible grief. I was silent while our dear friend shuddered with great heart-broken sobs.

During the following days when my father went to the creamery he would phone the hospital for news of Connie. The hospital was in Cork, which back then was considered to be a huge distance away. At the time, parents were not permitted to stay in hospital with their children, which must have been heart-breaking for my mother. Every morning she waited on the doorstep for my father to return from the creamery with news of Connie. The news was never good. One morning as we stood around her, waiting, he came slowly into the yard, paler than usual, and announced in a choked voice, 'It is all over.'

I did not feel any worse because it was if it had already happened. I actually felt better because I decided that now he had left the hospital and gone to heaven, he would be able to come back to me. Every day I checked the treehouse in case he was there. When this did not work out, I decided it was back to our bedroom he would come. Our little room had been stripped bare and a sulphur candle stood guttering and spluttering on our bedside table.

The nuns in the hospital had given my mother a relic of St Theresa in a waxen pink rose, which was also on the table. I hated that pink rose. In some way I had come to the conclusion that God had taken Connie and sent back this stupid rose. One day when I peeped in to see if Connie was there, I could stand it no longer, so I caught the rose and tore it up, petal by petal. To my mother, the relic and rose had been a comfort and I found it very difficult to explain to her why I had torn it asunder. Nothing was making any sense in this frightening new world.

The reality that Connie was gone forever was beyond my comprehension. I saved my sweets for him and when my mother mentioned visiting his grave I ran upstairs to collect the sweets – and Patsy – to bring them to him. I have no recollection when his death finally became reality for me.

Now, a lifetime later, in that room with the antique bed smelling of a sulphur candle, the seal on the trauma was finally dissolving. By then I had children much older than I had been when Connie died. Later that night, back at home, the memories of Connie's death were still winging back as if the smell had turned the key in a locked memory box. I sat on the side of my bed with tears running down my face and wrote a long poem. I was completing a grief journey that had been postponed for years. It was time for the buried tears.

Smell is one of the most evocative of the senses. It creeps like smoke back along the membranes of memory until it reaches its source. There it ignites a flame that melts down a time barrier; the past and present come together and we go back to the root of memory. At six I was unable to cope with the pain of parting from Connie, so nature stepped in to protect me.

Sometimes we can learn from nature as we observe how it deals with trauma. The bees in their hives are wise in their own way. When, as sometimes happens, a mouse breaks into the hive the bees simply cover him over with wax and render him powerless. He is a problem for another day. With time he may disintegrate and fade, or at a later date the wax may wear away and he will be still there, but by then easier to handle – he can be eased out as the bees clean the hive.

Now, as an adult, the wax coating over my childhood trauma melted away. I was in a good place to ease out the grief ghost that had slept for years, sealed off in my memory. Sometimes it is good to respect the wisdom of ages:

There is a time for everything
A season for everything under the sun.

The glow of Connie's memory has always been a little beacon of light and goodness in my life. His gentleness and playfulness was an oasis calling from my past. It caused me to be drawn to beautiful things and absorb the wonder in the ordinary.

A Memory

The waste ground was choked with weeds
That grew above her head,
But in the middle of this bloomed
A flower of golden red.

The little child came every day
To gaze upon the scene.
The flower was the loveliest sight
That she had ever seen.

This flower took root and blossomed.
It grew inside her head
And led her on to lovely things
Long after it was dead.

Chapter 2

The Comforter

Bill never criticised us. To him we were perfect. He loved us unquestioningly and we responded by loving him back. He had no children of his own so my brother Connie and I became his children and because he was not involved in the nuts and bolts of our actual rearing he was the perpetual Santa Claus in our lives. When my father had to enforce a certain amount of law and order into our scene we told my mother that she should have married Bill instead as he would have been a much kinder father, to which our father would caustically retort, 'You would all have died of the hunger.' But as children we only saw all that was wonderful in Bill.

We viewed him as the father figure who never stood in

judgement and who deemed us always to have only the most superior motives. He surrounded us with approval and support. The old *sean fhochail* '*Mol an óige and tiochfaid siad*' (Praise the young and they're yours) definitely applied to us. We blossomed in Bill's non-judgemental approval. He had gone to school with my father, who regarded him as a cross between a genius and a romantic fool not fit to survive the harsh realities of North Cork farming in the hungry 40s and 50s. My father's assessment was probably right, but to us Bill was a magic window into the fantasy world of the imagination. He loved reading and telling stories. The child in Bill had never grown up, so even though he was an adult he was never burdened with the cares of that world.

My father constantly tried to bribe and threaten him into eking out a better living on his hill farm so that he and his two sisters could live in more comfort, but Bill's heart was not in it and when every other farmer in the neighbourhood was busy saving their hay, Bill would be occupied reading a book or researching a new breed of *ciaróg*, or insect. This would drive my father crazy, but Bill would just ignore him and calmly go his own way, much to the annoyance of his disapproving sisters. Bill was never meant to be a struggling farmer; farming life would have suited him if he had had another source of income, but unfortunately that was not the case. However, because one of his sisters was thrifty and a good housekeeper, they managed. But he was the bane of her life and Bill lived to the sound of her scolding disapproval – though because it was constant, like background music, he never really heard it. Connie and I certainly ignored it and regarded her as a thorn in the side of Bill's happiness and our own.

Bill and his sisters lived at the top of the hill behind our house and the place was my escape from my own bossy sisters and the never-ending line-up of dreaded 'jobs'. When the pressure became too much I sneaked out through the grove behind our house and along a ferny field, and then hopped over the stream at the foot of the hill and climbed up the steep path beside the wooded fort, then ran along the Fort Field and over the ditch into the field in front of Bill's house. Here, Shep had to be confronted, and though we met daily, he never extended a warm welcome. He was a snarling mongrel who held his ground and kept me on top of the ditch until Bill called him off. But once he was called to heel it was all plain sailing after that. No matter what farming business he had on hand, Bill took time to sit and chat; there was no hurry at the top of the hill. His donkey was in perfect harmony with Bill's pace of life, and I loved to be there too when the cows came in for milking, picking their way carefully over Bill's uneven stone yard and then placidly chewing the cud as their heads protruded out through the thatched roof of their house – over the years the cows had gently butted holes into the thatch and formed their own windows so that as they were milked they gazed happily out over the adjoining fields. The thatch had weathered to a mellow grey and all the timber gates had softened too to the same hue; even the donkey was the same soft grey.

Every night Bill came to our house bringing a bucket of spring water from the fairy well at the foot of the fort on his land and when we calculated our water supply, Bill's bucket was always included. He was as constant as the northern star. The only night that he did not come was Saturday night as he knew that was bath night when we five sisters were scrubbed clean in a tin bath in front of the kitchen fire. Every other night he came, and then stayed and with endless patience taught us our lessons. Spelling was not my strong point and I recall one particular night when he spent hours trying to drum the spelling of 'immediately' into my meandering mind. He told us stories and taught us Irish dancing, which was some achievement as he was a big man, wearing heavy wooden clogs with iron tips, so the intricacies of the fairy reel did not flow easily. During the war years such footwear replaced hob-nailed boots in rural Ireland, but even with such restraints, Bill succeeded, with patience and determination, in teaching us the complications of Irish dancing. Sometimes the tip of his clog would come loose and it added an extra tempo to the rhythm!

At Christmas he played cards with us, and if anyone cheated he got very annoyed. When we were sent off to bed and could not settle down but started a bit of a racket over-head, he would come to the bottom of the stairs and warn us that our father's patience was wearing thin and that it was time to calm things down a little.

Like a kind of Santa Claus, Bill was large and ample, with a benevolent, beaming face shining with goodwill and kind-ness under a large bald head. He was always on our side.

When Connie died my mother was devastated and my father retreated into a frozen silence, but Bill remained a secure, unchanged rock in the middle of my sea of anguish. Bill provided normality then – and at that time we really needed something to remain the same in our shattered world. To me Bill was indestructible.

All his life Bill had suffered from bad asthma, which he treated by burning some strange substance in a tin box and inhaling it up his nostrils. I was fascinated by this procedure and would lean in over the box and try to sniff it up my nose, much to the annoyance of Bill's sisters. But even though Bill had asthma he was never really sick and always kept going at his own leisurely pace. Along his pathway up by the fort were little seats that he had cut into the hillside and made comfortable with flat stones. Here he rested regularly on his trek up the steep hill. That steep hill must have been a tough challenge for an asthmatic.

When he missed a few nights in bringing his bucket of water I wondered, but was not unduly disturbed. But the following Sunday, as my sister Ellen and I walked home from Mass, we made a detour and called to see him. Instead of being up in his usual loft bedroom which was accessed by a ladder, he was now in a big bed in what was called 'the upper room'. He did not talk and his heavy breathing filled the space. An icy finger of dread crept into my stomach. I came down the hilly field feeling a cold, hard knot forming at the base of my stomach. I went out into the grove and sat beside the tree where Bill had sat with me and cried on the night Connie had been taken away. I had not understood anything about death then. At that time I was six, now I was twelve and had learnt a little more. Later that day, Bill died. I did not want to go back up to that room where Bill's laboured breathing had filled the air.

The following evening when I knew that the hearse would be leaving his home I went up to a spot at the top of our farm that overlooked Bill's house. As the hearse drove across the field, the knot in my stomach grew into a big, cold lump. It was hard and painful. I was beginning to learn about the deep pain of grief.

The day after Bill's funeral one of his sisters came to my mother and asked if one of us would go and stay with them as they were so lonely without Bill. It was Easter and we had holidays from school. Maybe because I was the one who had always climbed the hill to their home I now returned there with a small bundle of clothes under my arm. But now everything was different. Without Bill, the light had gone out of this special place. One of the sisters, Ellie, was fastidious and fussy and supervised my every move. She was very bothered by her arthritis and spent most of the day sitting in a timber *súgán* armchair by the fire, from where she supervised all activities. Her hair was swept back severely into a tight knot at the back of her head and everything about her was exacting and correct. She was thin and severe – maybe years of pain had led to her strict attitude. Her small kitchen had become her little empire. The other sister was the exact opposite in that she was bedraggled and untidy, with long, unruly black hair, and she stomped around in a large pair of unlaced boots. The two sisters slept in a high, iron bed in the lower room and I climbed in between them. They wore long woollen nightdresses and smelt of Sloane's lineament, which they rubbed on themselves to relieve their aches and pains.

Every morning I was called and given exact instructions by Ellie on how to light the fire, starting with emptying the ash hole and then twisting up small bits of paper to create firelighters that were surrounded with little bits of soft turf called *ciaráns* and small pieces of wood we called '*cipíns*' that I had collected the previous day from under the trees in the haggard. Then I was instructed on exactly how many cups of water to put into the heavy kettle before hanging it on the iron hook of the crane over the fire. Ellie was like a time-and-motion expert, and I wondered if she too had the hard, cold lump in her stomach that I had.

When the hated jobs were done I walked around the little haggard, ran my hand along the smooth shafts of Bill's donkey cart and sat on the cow stool under the sagging roof of the cow shed. At the gable end of the house were the logs that Bill had brought from the wood and neatly stacked. Down along the little garden beside the house the daffodils were peeping above the ground. But without Bill the whole place was desolate.

When school reopened I was glad to go home to where nobody worried about how many cups of water you put into the kettle. But it took a long time to get used to the idea that Bill would never again come in our door carrying his bucket of water. My hillside haven was gone forever.

Years later, I read that wise man and wonderful writer, John O'Donoghue, who tells of an old neighbour whom he had loved dearly dying suddenly when he was a child. It was his first encounter with death and with it came a realisation that all the people around him had known about it all the time. To him as a child it was an enormous discovery and he was amazed that in the midst of this extraordinary happening people carried on and life continued almost normally around it. I too wondered how the world could continue without Bill. For months I walked up his hillside path and sat on his seats and thought about him. I had no idea why I did it. It hurt, but in some way it brought Bill closer. He was part of that hill. Gradually my world reshaped itself without him.

Chapter 3

Animal Friends

We grew up cloaked in post-war austerity and most parents during my childhood struggled to keep bread on the table. There was no surplus money for toys. But what we never had we never missed, and because children are by nature resourceful we found other sources of entertainment. Often the farm animals became our 'toys'. If baby *bonhams* and lambs needed special nursing, we were on standby to become Florence Nightingales. Chickens, goslings and ducklings brightened up the spring and in the summer we raced the baby calves down through the fields. But baby animals grow up quickly and move on, and so it was with the older animals that we formed the most lasting bonds.

We became very attached to the farm dogs and horses,

some of whom were older than ourselves. One of our horses, Paddy, was the same age as my older sister, Ellen, and I envied her that close affinity with him. It was as if they shared a special connection because of being born in the same year. Paddy was the king of the stable; other horses came and went, but Paddy seemed to go on forever.

We sensed too that my father had huge respect and love for Paddy. At that time, horses were one of the main cogs keeping a farm in motion. My father depended on Paddy to plough, harrow and cut the hay and corn. He was well cared for because without him there would be no food and in the working process of man and horse an inter-dependency developed and a close friendship that neither of them could articulate. Farmers were not into declaring their deepest feelings, but that is not to say that they did not exist. It was rather a case of care and share. There was a deep and silent understanding between my father and Paddy.

Paddy was a large bay who was by nature volatile, but he was a great worker and when he was out in the fields doing farm work that required a pair of horses, he was the one who set the pace: when two horses work together there is usually the pace-maker and the one who follows. During fine weather the horses were always out on the land, and every morning catching the horses was one of our first jobs of the day; one of us brought in the cows while another went for the horses. The horses did not always take kindly to being rounded up but usually a long, low whistle brought Paddy ambling in your direction and for some reason the other horses followed. The most troublesome was the small, sprightly jennet, whose job it was to go to the creamery. The jennet was a vindictive creature who would kick and bite if he got half a chance, but he never succeeded with us because on a farm the first rule of survival was to expect the unexpected. Instead of being street-wise we were country-wise.

In the stable too there was a pecking order, with Paddy occupying the main section, and next to him came Jerry, and then near the door the jennet, who was nameless as he was the only one of his kind on the farm, and indeed in the parish - therefore he remained simply 'the jennet'. Above their heads was a window through which hay could be thrown from the barn into their mangers during the winter months when they could not go out into the fields. But during the long days of summer, once their work was done, they were free to graze the fields behind the house and up along the Glen that stretched across the northern end of the farm. They must have known every inch of this territory, so it was difficult to understand how Paddy had his accident.

It was an early May morning when Ellen, who had gone to catch the horses, ran back to the house, breathless and panic stricken. Her announcement that Paddy had fallen down over a cliff up in the Glen triggered pandemonium. Everyone headed up for the Glen. Poor Paddy was lying at the bottom of a cliff, his eyes wide with terror. He whined piteously when he saw my father – it was almost as if there was a special communication between them and now he was asking his best friend for an explanation. But his friend had no answer.

That day I went to school with the horror of Paddy's predicament scorched into my mind. I knew by my father's face that morning that there was no easy way out of this calamity. I took in nothing that went on in school as Paddy's terrified eyes blotted out everything. The minute I got home I ran up to the Glen where he was still lying, and I knew then that there was no solution. If it had been possible to get him up, my father would have managed it. I soon found out that the vet had been called and had pronounced that Paddy had a broken back. It was a death sentence.

Later that evening as dusk was falling I went back up to the Glen and climbed down the steep incline. I rubbed poor Paddy's soft nose and he whimpered in distress. As I walked down the field blinded by tears, I saw my father come towards me carrying his gun. It would be the quickest and the kindest way for Paddy, but brutal for my father. I waited to hear the sound of the gun and when it did not come I realised that my father was waiting for me to reach home and be out of hearing range. But I sat on a stone in the middle of the Fort Field and waited. When the shot came, it tore through the silence of the night and echoed along the valley. Slowly my father came down the field and wordlessly I slipped my hand into his and we walked home together. Sometimes words are meaningless. Paddy was buried in the Glen and a certain sadness hung around his burial place ever after.

The following year one of our cows got sick and was nursed under a tree in the Quarry Field behind the house. When my mother approached with a bucket of warm bran the cow just mooed plaintively and lay there passively, her large, kind eyes full of questioning pain. She too was buried where she died under the tree at the top of that field, and for years afterwards when I walked into the Quarry Field I felt a haunting sadness waft around that tree too. Parting from animal friends can cause deep hurt because next to the bond between humans is the bond between man and animal.

Growing up on the land, we became aware very early in life that the birth and death of our animals was part of the natural order of life on a farm. We had to accept and develop a resilience to this way of life. The pattern of the seasons was the backdrop to the farming lifestyle, so we absorbed the rhythm and balance of nature and the need to respect the natural order. Out in the countryside you become conscious that you are only a very small part of the greater pattern of things and this awareness bred in us a respect for the balance of nature and an awe and love for the wonders of the countryside. The land is a hard taskmaster but the people who work it derive strength and a tenacity to keep going. I remember one November evening shortly after Paddy's accident, being sent with a jug of tea and two cuts of brown bread to my father who was up winter-ploughing in the Brake Field. When I went in the gap I stood and looked across the ploughed furrows at my father and his two horses silhouetted against the skyline of the sinking sun. Even as a child I sensed that I was looking at something special. It was the unity of man, God and nature. Out there, ploughing, my father was blending into the earth and finding redemption.

A Ploughed Field

Oh brown ploughed field
What an ancient skill
Is in your turned sod,
A skill inherited
By generations of country men
Beneath the sheltering trees
You cover the hillside
In a cloak of brown velvet.
What a softness is yours;
You are an open book
Yet to be written;
The virginity of the upturned sod
Waiting to be fertilised
By the hands of man
And nurtured by the warmth of nature.

Inner
Sanctum

Chapter 4

Thinking Time

He told us regularly, 'I'll be dead for years before ye realise what a wise man I am.' As children we thought it was a hilarious pronouncement, but now I realise that it was true. Some people are ahead of their time and are not really appreciated until time proves them right. Now, as I remember my father's wisdom and vision, I wonder how he was so far ahead. For him life was more challenging than it was for my mother who was fully occupied coping with the present as it unfolded. He was also impatient and quick-tempered, and expected everyone around him to move fast. We knew early in life that when he told you to do something he meant now and quickly. He certainly sharpened our reflexes.

Nature was his balm and daily he walked the fields of his

farm. For years I thought that he was out checking animals and boundary ditches, but as I grew older and a little wiser I realised that he just needed to get away from all of us. He had an easy-going wife and six children and often plenty of visitors too, and there were times when all the clatter around the house must have driven him to the outer regions of a nervous breakdown. The fields were his escape hatch and out there he regained his equilibrium; he always returned a calmer person. He had far more respect for nature than he had for his fellow human beings, and felt from experience that nature would never bring the disappointment he sometimes suffered from his fellow men.

We grew up being constantly instructed that one should never upset the balance of nature. He warned us that if people wronged nature there was a terrible price to be paid. Trees were of huge importance in his world; he planted many and would not lightly cut one down, and constantly reminded us that it took a tree decades to grow and that a fool could cut it down in five minutes. Even in those far-off days when water pollution was unheard of, he was constantly monitoring the streams and *glaishes* that found their way down the hilly slopes of our farm into the river in the valley below. It caused him great annoyance if my mother's ducks and geese were found swimming in the stream that ran through the Horse's Field and made the water unpalatable for the horses. In his book nobody, even in the animal world, impinged on the rights of another to fresh drinking water. At that time we drew most of our drinking water from the well in a field behind the house – supplemented by water from our neighbour Bill's 'fairy well'. An enamel bucketful always stood on the corner of the kitchen table. When my father came into the house during the day he always went to the dresser for a cup and helped himself from the water bucket, and last thing at night on his way upstairs to bed, he did likewise. In later years, on the one occasion in his life that he had to go into hospital, his one request was that a bottle of well water be brought to him as he considered the hospital water a health hazard.

The river that ran through the valley at the bottom of our farm brought him immense pleasure. Every summer Sunday when he came home from Mass, out came his rod and fishing tackle and then a complicated ritual of catching flies took place – this was done in a cow's horn covered with mesh wire. These were special flies that were foxy-coloured and long-tailed. If one of us was lucky enough to be allowed to accompany him on these almost sacred pilgrimages to the river we were under threat of extermination not to make noise lest we frighten the fish. I loved crawling along through the high ferns and watching the fish jump. For fear of distraction, we were never allowed to come close enough to watch the actual catch. But gradually the grey jute bag would fill up and he usually brought it home full of slippery brown trout. Then we sometimes wished that he had been less successful because it was our job to take the trout to the water spout at the bottom of the yard, then gut them and clean them out under the running water. But we had no such problem with large numbers when my mother cooked them in the bastable over the open fire and they reappeared sizzling and butter-soaked on the table.

Later in the year salmon came up that river to spawn and poachers went out late at night armed with a 'gaff' – a lit sod soaked in paraffin oil to dazzle the salmon and gaff them to their doom. My father took a poor view of this activity and when one unwary young neighbour brought us a gift of a poached salmon, my father promptly opened it up on the kitchen table and showed him and all of us the eggs, and spoke about the destruction of future fish life in the killing of this unwary salmon. We were never again given a poached salmon.

As it is today, the weather forecast was of huge importance to farmers and my father was a constant listener to weather forecasts on the radio. He was also a great observer of natural weather signs and of the night sky, and he had his own way of knowing if the following day was going to be sunny enough to cut the hay or the corn. The moon was very significant in his weather assessments and he never bought a calendar that didn't show the moon cycles. Often at night he would take us out and point out the varying angles of the moon and the location of different stars in the night sky. I loved my father most at these times when he seemed to be yearning heavenwards to an unknown realm that was way above and beyond our ordinary world.

The arrival of the swallows in spring brought him great delight and we children competed with each other to be the one to see the first swallow or to hear the first cuckoo. When cutting hay or corn he always watched out for nesting wildlife and often a patch remained uncut somewhere in the field until the baby birds were hatched out and had safely flown away. Once when a mother pheasant failed to return to the nest, her eggs were placed beneath one of our hatching hens, and they hatched out along with the chickens. He knew the name of every bird that visited the farm and sometimes at night as he sat by the fire he drew bird pictures in our school copybooks. Later, when the lessons were done and the rovers, as we called the visiting neighbouring farmers, were gone home, he would sit smoking his pipe, gazing into the fire. If asked then what he was doing he would nod his head slowly and tell you, 'Thinking.' But most of his thinking was done out in the fields from where he brought home early-morning mushrooms, blackberries and wild crab apples and where he ate haws as he walked along, declaring them to be very good for 'the system'.

As he grew old he grew more restful and then when you asked him as he sat by the fire smoking his pipe, 'What are you doing, Dad?' He would answer calmly, 'Waiting.' His journey was coming to a close and he was quite at ease with moving on. I often wondered where this total acceptance came from and came to the conclusion that it was from the farming way of life and his closeness to nature. He had witnessed the coming and going of the seasons and the yearly unfolding of the natural world around him. His animals had been bred, born, reared and died on his farm and he had journeyed with them; at one stage we had three generations of the same family of cows in the herd and they were almost as important as ourselves in the life of the farm.

He was not a praying man and regarded some of the religious practices of the time as daft, but he was very close to what he conceived his God to be – his God was out in the fields, and at a time when each Church went a separate road he would shake his head at the folly of it all and say, 'We are all going in the same direction.' He regarded big funerals as a crazy exercise, declaring them to be 'A queue of mad men following a dead man.' I think that he would have liked to die quietly in his own bed and be buried with minimum fuss under the trees in the orchard below the house. He got the first half of his wish because one night, after getting into his bed, he died quickly and quietly. His waiting was over.

His wake took place in the parlour where his wedding photograph and old photographs of his parents looked down on him. His was the sixth generation of his family to live in this house and two succeeding generations were now also gathered there. Friends and neighbours came to say goodbye and one old friend came with a mission in mind: he had come not to express the usual mundane sentiments but specifically to 'look upon' his old friend and see him off on his long journey. Ignoring us all, he made a beeline for my father's coffin and grasping both sides of it gazed down fondly for a very long time into the face of his friend of a lifetime. He was in no hurry; you cannot rush saying goodbye to eighty years of togetherness. Having dealt with the main matter, he finally got around to sympathising with my mother and the rest of us.

Later, as the hearse left the yard, it was as if we had come to the last chapter of a long story. After supper I walked down through my father's fields to his beloved river. He was gone, but his spirit was all around me in the gathering dusk of that February evening. The dark river was silent. Eight generations of his family had lived by this river that had flowed quietly through all our lives. It made me realise how transient we are and how timeless nature is. My father had found his God and his peace out here, and you could feel it in the night air.

The New Moon

You studied the night sky
Saw the future in the new moon
In the plough and in the stars.

You lived in a starry realm
That shone on a kind landscape
Where a new moon opened
A window to the milky way.

Now you have flown home
Towards that new moon
Up beyond the plough
And the stars.

Your wings opened
On the milky way
As you soared
Unfettered into a
New morning.

My Father

Now that you are gone
My father . . .
What is left behind?
The heritage you left us
Was the treasures
Of your mind.

Goldsmith was your
Special friend
You'd quote him
Verse by verse
I quoted him for you
As I walked behind
Your hearse.

You planted trees
Upon your land
And lived to see
Them grow.
A man who needlessly
Cut a tree
You did not
Want to know.

And Time Stood Still

On all the birds
Upon your land
You could
Put a name
You knew their
Natural habitat
From whence
And where
They came.

Honesty was
Your creed in life
You gave more
Than was due
But never expected
Anyone to do
The same for you.

These are all the gifts
My father
You have left behind
The greatest
Gift of all
A philosophy of mind.

Chapter 5

The Woman of the House

One of the idiosyncrasies that I have inherited from my mother is that I cannot face a mug on the breakfast table. She believed that a cup and saucer were prerequisites to any partaking of tea. It was not that she was into posh living, but she believed that both people and food deserved to be treated with a certain amount of decorum. We grew up in a house where frugal living was the order of the day, but my mother was of the opinion that 'being without fostered the art of making do'. She was not into 'house beautiful', but could put a gloss on meagre provisions; good food was her top priority and a properly laid-out table was necessary for the comfort and wellbeing of her diners, be they the immediate family, neighbours or visiting relations. She had married into a long-tailed family in an old farmhouse on a hillside farm near the Cork–Kerry border from where, out of necessity, previous generations had emigrated all over the world. But though we Irish may have wanderlust in our blood, the tug of our roots is also very strong, so, like the salmon in the river at the bottom of our farm, shoals of Taylor descendants constantly returned to visit the ancestral home and she always welcomed them back wholeheartedly to their home place. They were entertained to tea in the parlour and stories of their ancestors. She had a better knowledge of my father's family tree than he had, and sometimes had more welcome for his extended family too! A staunch believer in family traditions, she was a cornerstone in his family as well as her own. She often told us that to denigrate your husband's family is to denigrate your husband – years later the memory of that bit of wisdom often kept my mouth shut! Her one good linen tablecloth and the set of fine china that she had inherited from my grandmother appeared not only when the Stations were held in our house and at Christmastime, but for all special visitors throughout the year.

But there were feasts outdoors too. When we were saving the hay she made a big, juicy apple cake to be eaten out in the meadow and no matter what mayhem was taking place in the kitchen her first priority was to feed the workers in the field. Saving hay was sweaty, hard labour and we complained about hay seeds down our backs and unexpected briars scratching our legs and encounters with moist frogs who made surprise appearances, but when we caught sight of my mother coming down the hilly field from the house carrying a basket which we knew contained apple cake, and a white enamel bucket full of tea, we forgot all our complaints. We loved tea in the meadow and when we voiced our appreciation of the apple cake she would smile modestly and tell us, 'Hunger is a wonderful sauce.'

With her great sense of occasion she turned Christmas into a magical experience. Children love a swell of expectation and being involved in all the preparations. We were expected to be part of the Christmas clean-up and then it was our job to go to the wood for holly and decorate the house. It never bothered her when, in our childish exuberance, we turned the kitchen into a replica of the nearby grove – as long as she had red-berried holly for the Christmas candle and potatoes boiled to stuff the goose on Christmas Eve, all was well in her world. She was never annoyed by excited children dragging holly branches around her feet and she calmly sorted out stand-up fights when they arose – all this palaver drove my father crazy and he would disappear until the kitchen was decorated to our satisfaction and peace restored. A staunch believer in God and family traditions, she loved Christmas and wove such a spiritual essence into all the celebrations that we children considered the crib to be as important as Santa Claus. A devotee of the nightly family rosary, she brought us all to our knees for the ritual, though when her extra prayers or 'trimmings' got out of hand my father would complain, 'Ah Missus, we'll be here till morning' – her title always changed from 'Lena' to 'Missus' when she over-stepped his threshold of tolerance.

She was a natural cook and led me to the belief that one of the primary ingredients in good cooking is love of people. She loved us all and nothing was too good for us, or for any of her visitors. A firm conviction that everyone was as good as they could be was her central creed in life, which often caused my father to raise his eyes to heaven at the absurdity of such thinking.

The fox was the only creature that drew her ire – he was the bane of her life when he raided her sheds on his nocturnal visits and deprived her of well-fattened ducks and geese. He and she competed to feed their young, she would agree, but his wanton killing, just for the sake of it, was what she could not forgive. When in later years I took up painting and told her that I loved painting foxes, she assured me that if I had had the experience of them that she had there would be no love lost between us!

She was the perfect grandmother as she showered her grandchildren with unconditional love which they lapped up like cats a saucer of cream. When she came to visit our house she fulfilled all their culinary requests and they savoured creamy tapioca and semolina puddings that their mother failed to produce. On annual family visits to Ballybunion she accompanied them nightly to 'the merries' and constantly replenished pockets rapidly emptying from swingboat rides and turns in the bumpers.

Old age came to her with grace and dignity, and she had the innate ability to gently correct and pass on her wisdom without insulting the recipient. Once in a reflective moment she told me, 'I regret now that I mourned Connie for so long.' This remark about my little brother who had died aged six surprised me and on further discussion she told me that she now felt that she had got bogged down in grief, and that that was a big mistake. 'Grief can suck the life out of you,' she said, and once you have grieved for a certain amount of time she thought that you must make a big effort 'to try to go forward because you can't live your life looking backwards.' The years had brought her tranquility and acceptance of his death. Later I read similar thoughts in the words of Cardinal Basil Hume when he said that 'Grief will yield to peace – in time.'

Having pondered on the suddenness of my father's death, she smiled when I assured her, 'If Dad was confined to bed for any length of time he would have eaten a hole out through the wall.' She herself, however, was confined to bed for two years as the result of a stroke before she died. It seemed a harsh end for someone who had moved gently and calmly through life. It makes one wonder about the biblical quote: 'As a man lives so shall he die' – my father got out fast, she took it slowly.

Those years after the stroke were difficult. My mother became the cared for, instead of the carer. Caring for the elderly at home is a demanding and energy-draining business and though we rotated the caring, the one who really bore the brunt of it was my sister, Phil, who proved to have sterling qualities in the field. We all went through periods of frustration and exhaustion but Phil kept us all focused and we coped because our mother would have been unhappy in any place other than her beloved Lisdangan. She who had done so much for all of us deserved that. Then, early one August morning, she closed her eyes quietly and said goodbye to the home where for decades she had been the heartbeat.

I have never had the experience of having to fly home for a parent's funeral but I imagine that it must be fairly difficult. By the time my sister, Ellen, flew in from Toronto our mother's coffin was already in the church. Ellen and I went directly there from the airport and sat beside our mother for a long time; it was then I discovered that time to absorb the reality of death is very important. Then, very softly, Ellen began to sing one of our mother's favourite hymns and together we sang many of the hymns that we had grown up with and that would have been part of our mother's life. It was strangely comforting; I feel there is great healing in music and song. Later that day we sang them again at her funeral Mass in the church where she had been baptised, received her First Holy Communion and was married. Her journey was complete. She was laid to rest with my father and Connie.

Afterwards we walked around the graveyard and chatted with our friends and neighbours. Taking time to visit the surrounding graves on the occasion of a family funeral in some way links the past with the present and makes us aware that we are part of a long chain of unfolding events. Old graveyards tell our story and the Taylor headstones in that graveyard date back to 1670. There are surprises too that comfort us at these times: I was pleasantly surprised to meet a friend from Innishannon who had never met my mother but years previously had actually painted her portrait. He had seen her photograph on the piano in our house and later had painted her from his memory of the photograph. It touched and comforted me that he had travelled so many miles to her funeral. It's the unexpected acts of kindness that help at such a time. Now he said: 'Having painted her, even though we never met, I felt that I knew her. She had a great face.'

Her going left a gentle sadness and a feeling that home

would not be home anymore. She had a long and contented life and died at harvest time when the corn was ripe. She left in us all a love of gardening and in me an inability to face a mug first thing in the morning. And beside my kitchen sink I have a little tin green soap dish with a pink flower on the cover – it had been part of her bedroom set for visitors. It is nice to remember those we have loved and who have loved us in the use of things they valued in life.

Chapter 6

The Listener

The friends thou hast, and their adoption tried,
Grapple them to thy soul with hoops of steel

William Shakespeare

I n life we all need a listener. Con was a good listener. He was also my 'Johnny sound all' in that if I was undecided on a course of action I ran it past him and he invariably sorted me out, mainly, I think, because he was totally non-judgemental and fair-minded and always delivered a balanced and well-thought-out opinion. We were of the same family tree in that our great-grandmothers were sisters, and this was the reason that he came to our house.

As a newly qualified maths and science teacher he got a job in St Brogan's school in nearby Bandon. On hearing this an old neighbour of his told him, 'There is one of the Taylors married up there so call in and she will look after you.' And that is exactly what happened – only instead of us looking after him, he looked after us.

By an odd coincidence Con had been born the year that my brother, Connie, had died and in some strange way when he came into my life he filled the shoes of the brother I had lost as a child.

The initial arrangement was that he would stay for a week until he found a more convenient place in Bandon – but he stayed for almost thirty years and became one of us. At the time we had a summer guesthouse and over winter we had three young girls who were teaching in local schools staying with us. It was a busy household, with staff from our adjoining shop sharing our kitchen table too, and neighbours coming and going. My husband, Gabriel, was part of everything that moved in the parish so ad-hoc meetings were often held at our kitchen table or in the '*seomra ciúin*' – the 'quiet room', as we called one of the front rooms which was devoid of TV and telephone. We had four small boys who added to the general mayhem, but Con, in his calm, quiet way, introduced an oasis of tranquility into our busy household.

Then one day a swarm of bees found their way into the

garden and so Con became a beekeeper. A range of hives soon stood in a row against the wall of an old hall at the top of our large garden. This old hall had once been a Wesleyian preaching hall and now its ivy clad, south-facing stone wall provided a sheltering backdrop for the hives. Con had the perfect temperament for a beekeeper in that he was patient, fastidious and had a delicate touch. During his long summer holidays he turned the back porch into a carpentry shop and made his own hives with painstaking precision. At extraction time, he gloried in the different shades of honey produced from clover, whitethorn and the other wild flowers that provided the nectar for honey of varying colours. After he had supplied all and sundry, his honey was sold in the shop and demand always outran supply.

The same happened with the lettuces that he grew in a polytunnel at the top of the garden. He and Uncle Jacky, who lived next door and was a wonderful gardener, had long discussions in the garden about compost; and Jacky's wife, Aunty Peg, and Con often shared a quiet drink in her little sitting room behind the shop. He was with us during the long months of home nursing that preceded both their deaths and his understanding stretched to encompass the idiosyncrasies of Peg's sister, Aunty Min, who also lived out her last days with us – when she insisted on turning off the TV during an All-Ireland final so that everyone could focus properly on the meal she had made, he was the one who prevented war from breaking out. He was in the kitchen too when the shock announcement came of my brother-in-law Bill's death and again when the phone call about Uncle Jacky's death came from Dun Laoghaire. Con was part of the family scaffolding that held us all together.

Aunty Peg always regretted the fact that we had no girl in the family so when after her death I became pregnant and a little girl duly arrived I felt that she was sent by Aunty Peg. After four boys it was great for Gabriel to have a daughter! Con became a foster parent and over the years the two of them were inseparable. She was christened Lena Síle Mairéad after her two grandmothers and Aunty Peg, but Con always called her Lindy – and as soon as she could talk he became Condy. They had a very special relationship.

He was a great craftsman, especially in wood. When Lena was able to grasp the idea of Santa, he made her a fine big doll's house that provided years of play; he showed it to me on the morning of that Christmas Eve when he and I went to an old cottage he was restoring outside the village where he put the finishing touches to it – it was many years before she discovered that Con was the Santa who had crafted her wonderful doll's house. Then when our kitchen table, which I had inherited from my sister, Theresa, began to fall asunder he made us a solid wooden table that defied the assault of stampeding teenagers.

He and Lena often went to the seaside when she could

just waddle into the water and as she grew older he took her book shopping, and they shared a deep interest in the *Titanic*, which led to the buying of many books on the subject.

He loved books. Fine, well-bound books were his one big extravagance in life and I enjoyed buying books with him as it was an exercise in sheer self-indulgence in one who was by nature very restrained. First, of course, the book had to be on a chosen subject, but that could be anything from ancient European history to astrology, so wide were his interests. He would open up the book and examine the binding; the stitching had to be perfect – glued books were dismissed on the spot. Then he examined the quality of the paper and he ran his finger along its spine and finally he smelt its interior. It was almost as serious an undertaking as buying a horse.

When Lena took up horse-riding he ferried her back and forth to the stables and never objected when on the eve of a competition he had to watch television surrounded by smelly tackle as she polished it around his feet – her brothers had no such tolerance and threatened her with eviction, but Con backed her up, and if things were the other way she was always in his corner. During her secondary school years he dropped her off at her convent school on his way to St Brogan's. They chose her school subjects together and decided on her university course. Two of the boys went to his school and as they all grew up he was the peace-maker who often sorted out family squabbles. Gabriel and he were bridge partners and sometimes held bridge sessions in the *seomra ciúin*. Later, my sister, Ellen, decided to join them when she first came to over-winter in Innishannon to avoid the harsh Canadian climate.

It was on her arrival for Christmas one year that Con had what we considered a bad 'flu, but as he was on school holidays he could take it easy and we were not unduly worried. But Ellen, who was a nurse, insisted on a visit to the doctor, who sent him to the hospital for tests. We thought it was routine, but when we were summoned to meet the consultant it sent shock waves through the house.

Con's brother, Fr Denis, who is also a doctor, came from Dublin and together with Con we met the consultant in a little office down the corridor from Con's room. He imparted a death sentence. The news was devastating. There was no question of the reprieve of an operation and the time was short. It was a bolt from the blue and we were shattered. Out in the corridor a doctor from the hospice waited to talk and offer hospice care, but Con opted to come home.

Denis and I drove back to Innishannon in stunned silence and Ellen was waiting for us in the kitchen. Our faces told the story. Gabriel came in and we all discussed how best to make things as easy as possible. Denis being a doctor and Ellen a nurse, we had the medical know-how to take care of

Con at home. We also needed a shower off his bedroom, and his friend Liam, who taught with him in Brogan's, began to fit it that very evening.

Telling Lena was a terrible ordeal. All her life, he had been her friend and mentor and was, in many ways, like a third parent. She loved him as much as she did Gabriel and myself. At the time she was a first-year student in University College Cork, his old university, which is beside the hospital, so she was able to be with him during those early days. Con was one of five brothers, who, like Con, are wise, gentle people. Two of them are Redemptorist priests – Fr Denis and Fr Pat – and over the years they had often visited and now were coming for Christmas. Ellen, Lena and I got the house ready for Christmas in the usual way – we wanted Con when he came home to find it no different from other years. So he came back to a house with the crib, the tree, and candles waiting to be lit. He sat by the fire in the *seomra ciúin*, his usual calm self, and his close friends from St Brogan's came to visit him there.

On Christmas Eve we all gathered around to light the Christmas candle and as usual we sang 'Silent Night'. It could have been an ordinary Christmas. But it was not. We were all aware that this was Con's last one with us. We tried to be as normal as possible because the last thing that Con would have wanted was drama. But inside all of us our hearts were bleeding. We knew that we were balancing on top of an emotional precipice. That night Denis and Pat said the midnight Mass in our village church up the hill and the word quickly got around as to why they were here. It was a night filled with grief, grace and spirituality.

On Christmas morning Denis and Pat celebrated Mass in the kitchen and Con did one of the readings. It was a beautiful but heart-wrenching occasion when pain opened crevices in the mind and made it impossible to block our thoughts of things to come. Later, during the dinner, Con was able to take part in all that was going on and that night he held his own in our usual card game of A Hundred and Ten. You could almost convince yourself that maybe we might still have time. I got it into my head that as May was Con's favourite month he would be there for the beginning of the bee-keeping year.

After Christmas, Denis returned to Dublin to make arrangements to come longterm to Innishannon – but there was to be no longterm in it. The following morning Con's breathing became problematic and he was rushed to hospital. His brothers returned and a bedside vigil began. It lasted just a few days and on the night he eased slowly out of our world Denis quietly stood by his bed and said this beautiful and meaningful death prayer:

Go Forth, O Human Soul

Proficiscere, anima Christiana, de hoc mundo!
Saints of God, come to his aid!
Come to meet him angels of the Lord.
Go forth upon thy journey, O faithful Christian soul,
Go forth from this world; from your family, your friends, your home.
In the name of God the Father who created you and gave you life,
In the name of Jesus the Son of Mary who gave his life for you,
In the name of the Holy Spirit of God who was poured into your
*   heart.*
May your home this day be in paradise with the angels and saints
And with your own people who have gone before you on the great
*   journey.*
May you see the face of the living God.
May you have the fullness of life and peace for ever.
May Jesus the gentle shepherd number you among the faithful ones
And bring you to the waters of peace.
May you have eternal rest.

Amen.

It was all over. Con died as he had lived, with the minimum of fuss. The undertaker from his home village came
and prepared him for the journey back from Cork to Inn-

ishannon. Just before dawn Denis and I followed the hearse out the now deserted road and Gabriel had the front door open in readiness to receive him. We placed his coffin in the corner where over the years he had played chess with Lena, corrected school examination papers and had done the *Irish Times* crossword.

Some of our near neighbours gathered in. We knelt and said the rosary. The rosary at such a time is a calming, unifying prayer and its repetitive nature acts as a mantra to soothe the spirit. In the presence of death, words are meaningless and silence comes naturally in moments of deep sorrow.

But the following day the room filled with talk and that too had its place as his teaching friends and neighbours from his home village gathered. It had all happened so quickly that most of his fellow teachers and his pupils were taken completely unawares. His young students, who had parted with him for the Christmas holidays, now looked into his coffin with stricken faces. Death takes us all by surprise, but most of all the young. That night as the lid went on his coffin sobbing filled the room. My heart bled for Lena.

His pupils formed a guard of honour as his brothers and then our boys carried his coffin up the hill behind the house to the waiting hearse. It was a cold, starry January night as we followed it along the road back through Macroom and Carrianimma to the village of Boherbue where he had grown up. The following morning after Mass said by his brothers, he was laid to rest beside his parents. Our great-grandmothers had brought us together and over the years he had enriched our home with many blessings.

When we came home that night and walked in the back door I looked at all of Con's unused medicines that were stacked away neatly on a small table in the corner of the back porch. A blind rage filled me at the uselessness of all these little boxes. I threw them on the floor, crying with frustration and temper. I picked them up and banged them down on the table with venom. What a lot of useless rubbish they had proved to be! My anger had come like a burst dam. Then slowly it drained off. I sat down, exhausted, and cried for a long time.

The days after a funeral are brutal. You are like someone after major surgery where all your insides have been carved up. Our coping skills are non-existent and it seems impossible to find the healing road. It is good then to have understanding, loving people around us – God save us from the 'know alls' who think that they have the answers, and the 'wet blankets' who just want to drown us in their own sorrows. We need a listener. Ellen and I talked for hours.

My sister, Phil, came and brought my mother's sewing machine. It may seem like an odd thing to do, but in some strange way it helped. We sewed together in the warm kitchen. In grief you are somehow perpetually cold. Then Phil dragged me out into the garden where we dug and pruned, and where initially I just felt like lying down on the bare earth and crying. After days of pruning I looked around at the barren garden and thought: you are just like me, cut to the bone.

Then I was haunted by 'if onlys'. Why had I not seen that he was so ill? Of course, I encountered the 'experts' who told me that they had noticed that he was not looking well for months! Why had *I* not noticed? Why had I not looked after him better? Why? Why? Why? And, of course, there was no answer to all this self-flagellation.

I would not have touched Con's things for months, but the school wanted some of his papers because he normally prepared the timetable and the details were stored amongst his things. So, of necessity, the sorting-through began – but it was too soon. In all these things you need time. Going through someone's possessions after their death is a crucifying exercise and before you begin you need time to heal.

Afterwards

His room
A book
The story
Of his life.
Each crevice
Filled to capacity,

A beehive
Of remembrances.
A collector
Of coins
Family history
Rare books
And stamps.
His room
As his life
A book of interest.
I turned back
The pages of his life
Back to his childhood
This man's treasure
His love of little things
I walked on sacred ground
Back through his years.

Then my sister, Theresa, decided to visit her son who was living in Paris, and Gabriel, Ellen and I went with her. For me it proved not to be a good idea. The bereaved are better at home, I think. Many years previously at Listowel Writers' Week, Brian McMahon had told me so: after the death of his wife he had gone to America and he had discovered that it had simply postponed the grieving and made it more difficult. He was right.

I walked around Paris in a haze of pain. On the evening of our arrival we took a boat trip down the Seine and I sat at the back so that the others would not see the tears streaming down my face. In normal circumstances a visit to the Musée d'Orsay to view the Impressionist paintings would have filled me with delight, but now these paintings simply swam in front of me.

All except one. I came upon a painting that stopped me in my tracks: it was of a lone, bowed figure struggling through a snow blizzard. It captured aloneness and misery. There I saw myself and in that instant the artist and I were on the same wavelength. Such is the power of creativity, be it art, music, or poetry, it can span ages and link people across decades and divides. I never forgot that painting.

Later in Notre Dame cathedral the powerful organ thundered out its crashing notes and drowned my sorrow in its intensity. There is something in powerful music that can temporarily seal off the anguish of the soul. I sat there and looked across at the opposite pew and saw a mother and daughter. I knew by their faces that they too were bereaved: the bereaved have faces haunted with sorrow.

The day we came back to Innishannon we opened the door to the smell of home cooking and a great fire warmed the *seomra ciúin*. Theresa's daughter, Eileen, was there to welcome us home. I sat beside the fire and wept tears of relief to be home. This was the place to heal and put myself back together again.

For months after Con's death I had a strange dream. I was sitting on the shore of a lake holding a rope that was attached to a boat on the water, and Con was sitting in the boat. Slowly, over the months, the dream faded and then came no more. Did it fade as I accepted the reality of Con's death, I wondered?

Vacancy

He lived in the midst of us,
A quiet presence with a listening ear.
When he went an icy wind
Blew through the days
That he had filled with his kindness.

Brown Poultice

Easter Saturday
Still in the tomb,
Thorns embedded
In my mind.

And Time Stood Still

On a hard hill
Outside the village
We planted trees.
Dug deep holes
In freezing sleet.
Back-breaking work.
But into the holes
Ran raw pain
That became absorbed
Into brown earth,
And the kind earth
Poulticed my wounds.

Chapter 7

A Man for All Seasons

You were unburnished gold
That polished warm
With the living years:
I had loved you
With a young girl's
Delectable fancy,
But the wise-ing years
Revealed your inner depth.

Marriage is a bit like backing a horse in the Grand National: you can follow your hunches and study the odds, but you are half-way around the course before you know whether or not you have backed a winner. By then you have struggled over a few fences, cleared some and fallen at a few, and have tested your ability to rise and fall together. You have borne nights of exhaustion with crying babies, when heavy tiredness clings you to the bed. Both sets of parents have mingled and you have got to know your partner's extended family, and you have seen how all parties blend together.

Becoming part of another family is like grafting a new rose onto original stock. Grafting is a delicate operation – some grafting enhances the original stock and some depletes it. When the combination is good, you finish up with a well-rooted, balanced tree, where new shoots have all-round support and can withstand subsequent life storms.

Initially, Gabriel's adoptive mother, Aunty Peg, felt that I needed a bit of straightening out – and she was probably right, though I did not appreciate it at the time. However, his adoptive father, Uncle Jacky, thought that I was great, which, of course, endeared him to me from the beginning! Looking back now I realise that I was a bit of a prima donna, who was very taken up with appearances and with looking good. I also thought that Gabriel's place was at my side as a kind of 'permanent admirer' and I would very likely have turned into what one of my friends terms a 'grow-off-the-arm job' – but Gabriel was having none of it. Being part of all parish activities meant that he was out most nights at meetings. At first I resented it. I wanted an extended fan club, but he needed a wife who could stand on her own two feet.

Clinging

Do not cling
To me
As ivy
To a tree,
Draining my strength,
Growing nothing
Of your own;
Stand tall and free,
Then we will grow
As two strong trees
Sheltering each other,
Our roots intertwining.

That first year was a learning curve for me and later I was very grateful to Gabriel that he had the moral fibre to withstand my emotional blackmail. To Uncle Jacky and Aunty Peg he was the golden boy, and my mother, when she got to know him, joined the admiration society. He was kind and broad-minded and welcomed all my family with open arms. They all thought that he was wonderful and one forthright sister assured me: 'You were pure useless until you married Gabriel; he made a great job of you' – a sentiment that I strenuously rejected but secretly knew contained an element of truth.

From Gabriel I learned that the greatest gift you can have in a marriage is freedom. He was generous and impulsive and when there was a quick decision to be made he never hesitated, whereas I am a bit of a ditherer.

However, he did have one big fault. He was a crazy driver and in today's world would be tied to the kitchen table with a string of penalty points. He went to matches with tiers of young fellows, including some of our own, lining the boot and back seat. If Cork was beaten in the All-Ireland Final we scorched home in silence down the Naas dual carriageway at breakneck speed with my blood pressure registering as high as the car speedometer.

He loved challenges and we spent many years extending old buildings, and if I ever got a fanciful idea but considered it a half-risky prospect, he would sweep aside my reservations and encourage me to go for it. He would actually convince you that you were able to do anything.

Because you believed
I would light up your life
I did.

Because you believed
I could do anything
I did.

Because you think
I am filled with love
I am.

Because you think
I am beautiful
I am.

Because you know
I will walk on water
I will.

Because you know
I will reach for the stars
I will.

Love enabled me
To do the undoable
To reach the unreachable
To attain the unattainable.
It was the combination
That unlocked the vault
Hidden within.

When I took up writing he was unstinting in his support, never resenting the intrusion into his privacy, graciously receiving anyone who called, and was highly amused when he was referred to as Mr Taylor – we joked that when I came to live in the village I was known as 'Gabriel's wife' and now he was 'Mr Taylor'!

He worked long hours and was up very early every day to take in the post and morning papers. He was a great walker too, covering five or six miles daily. Because he loved Innishannon, he gave huge commitment to the Tidy Towns competition and often in the early hours before opening the shop, he went litter-picking around the village. When a bridge club was formed in the parish he took to it like a duck to water and played a few nights weekly.

But early one November morning all this activity crashed to a halt when, having got up to take in the papers, he collapsed on the shop floor. He was rushed to Cork University Hospital, and my sister, Ellen, and I accompanied him in the ambulance. But he never regained consciousness. For two days we sat with him, hoping and praying for a recovery while the family gathered from various locations – and then it was all over.

The room
Is cloaked in
After-death
Stillness.
He is gone into
Impenetrable
Sacred silence.
We are left
Standing
On the edge
Of a great mystery.

I would have liked to have brought Gabriel home with us to Innishannon immediately as we had done with our dear friend Con, but this was a different hospital with different procedures, so in the small hours of the morning we came back to Innishannon alone. We gathered around the *seomra ciúin* fire. It was time to cry, talk, and think about the funeral. Then to the funeral home to pick out a coffin where, due to shock and exhaustion, coffins swam before my eyes.

Later that morning we met the hearse at the old railway

Viaduct on the Bandon road just west of the hospital and from there followed Gabriel home to the village. The boys took the coffin into the front room, where the lid was removed. He could have been sleeping peacefully. Laid out in his good grey suit, wearing his precious *fáinne* – for proficiency in the Irish language – his pioneer pin, indicating total abstinence, and his GAA Gaelic Athletic Association tie. All his life he had been a stalwart GAA man, and held every officership in the local and divisional clubs, and he had refereed all his life. Now, at the final whistle, he had left the pitch running.

All day friends and neighbours gathered and some took over the kitchen while a constant supply of cakes and other food came in the back door. Good neighbours formed a comforting support system around us. Gabriel had been a central part of this community and now they came and the story of his life was retold around his coffin in the replaying of matches and village stories. All his life he had run the village shop and post office and as a young fellow had delivered telegrams around the parish, so he knew every family and was familiar with every boreen. The old friends came from the four corners of the parish. He had also been the one to welcome the people in the new estates, so they too filtered in, at first reluctant in case they were intruding, as many were not familiar with the concept of a country wake. Over the years many of the young people of the parish had worked in the shop and they came, remembering his kindness and the fun they had as they experienced their first holiday job.

I felt that I was walking around in a bubble of unreality. It was as if I was outside myself watching someone else talking and shaking hands with people. A wake is full of sadness, but in an unexplainable way it helps and gives time for the reality of what has happened to soak into deep crevices of the mind. There is so much about death that is beyond human understanding that when it comes we are walking in the dark. It is of such enormity that it is almost too much for the mind to absorb; some part of us goes into auto pilot, but in the undercarriage of the mind another scene is playing itself out.

But we also need silence and time alone to absorb the enormity of what has happened. That night some of us went to bed for short sessions and the neighbours held vigil. The following day dragged on – and I did not want the evening to come because with it would come the final departure from the house. But come it did, and with it the final closing of the coffin.

After the rosary people filed out until only his family remained around Gabriel. My heart bled for Lena and the boys – their father had a huge capacity for loving and nobody would ever again love them as much as he had. When the undertaker put the lid on the coffin I felt that everything that had made my life worthwhile was under it.

The four boys shouldered the coffin out the door and

along the street and then the Valley Rovers GAA members took him up the hill to the church. As the lit church came into view a strange peace came to me. Gabriel had loved this place and had come here to Mass every morning. He had worked hard for its recent restoration and now it was in pristine condition to receive him.

Then began the customary shaking of hands by everyone present, with the utterance of 'Sorry for you troubles.' I have always had slight reservations about this Irish practice because sometimes it seems a meaningless exercise, though when it comes with real feeling is a comfort. One young lad came and wordlessly gave my son, Mike, who was his team trainer, a strong hug; the boy was unable to articulate his feelings, but he wanted to bring comfort – and he did. Little things like that are a balm to frazzled minds.

Mass the following day was strangely beautiful and brought me comfort. Fr Pat was with us, but Fr Denis was in America and out of contact. During the Christmas of Con's death Gabriel had given Pat a copy of Dineen's Irish dictionary and taught him the prayers for Mass in Irish. Now Pat was here to say Mass in the language that Gabriel had loved so well. He gave an uplifting talk about the need to mourn and accept death, but also to link into the spiritual journey that Gabriel was now on. My niece, Treasa's wonderful voice poured out a haunting rendering of the 'Pie Jesu'. Its pathos filled the church and connected in a powerful way with the end of Gabriel's life. It brought a realisation that the separation of the soul from the earthly body is a huge wrenching, beyond all human understanding. The piteous agony of the song captures the trauma of that deep suffering. It had until then been beyond my understanding. Deep sorrow opens gaps into unexpected moments of grace and beautiful church music calms the mind and connects us to unreachable realms.

As the church bell tolled, the coffin, escorted by members of his bridge club, was taken down to Uncle Jacky and Aunty Peg's grave; as Gabriel was lowered into the earth I thought: the next coffin in there will be mine.

When the grave was covered Treasa led us all in singing Gabriel's favourite song, 'Carrigdhoun'. He loved that song and whenever we drove through the valley of Carrigdhoun he would break into it and at the same time, when the children were small, slow the car down so that they could see the white horse painted on a high rock there.

We returned to an overflowing house where the 'kitchen staff' had everything under control. It was a day of talk, crying and comforting, and if an observer had looked in the window it would have seemed like a big family get-together. But the heart of the family was gone and we had a long, hard road ahead of us.

The days after a funeral have to be endured to be understood; as Ellen was fond of saying, 'You must walk in the shoes.' I was so lucky to have my beloved sister with me then.

We talked, baked and cried together. It is so good if you have someone on the same wavelength to walk with you on the grief road. But it has to be someone who is in total harmony with your soul. For some unknown reason I got the notion that I would take up knitting and in an unexplainable way I found that sitting by the warm fire, knitting, somehow eased my pain. What I knit was a mess, but that did not matter. In grief there is no anticipating what will help. On the advice of a friend who had walked the same road, every day I lit the fire in the *seomra ciúin* and sat beside it. In grief you are chilled to the marrow of your bone and the warmth of a fire helps thaw you out.

Christmas was fast approaching and I dreaded it. One night, while meandering around the quiet house, I opened a little-used press and found that Gabriel had all our Christmas presents hidden in there, wrapped up and ready. As well as that, he had always bought canvases for 'Little Christmas' – or 'Women's Christmas', 6 January – for Ellen and myself, and they too were ready and lined up. It shook me to my foundations!

A few days before Christmas, while alone in the house, I decided to set up the crib. The lighting for the crib had always been Gabriel's job as I am not an electrical whizz kid, but that night everything worked splendidly and as the crib took shape a sense of peace soaked into my being and I just knew that we would be all right for Christmas.

On Christmas night after midnight Mass, Lena and I walked along the deserted village and over to the river where we leant over the bridge and watched the silent water. Silent water calms the anguish of the mind. Later that night I listened to thinker and sage John O'Donoghue's CD on the meaning of death which is part of his 'Beauty, the Invisible Embrace' collection. I'd had these CDs for several weeks and had listened to all the others but had been almost afraid to play this particular one; now, in some trepidation, I put it on. I was apprehensive about what it would do to me but something drove me on to listen to it, and I found it comforting. I have since played it many times and found great solace in it.

Often, then, I dreamt of Gabriel and in the dream he was alive and with us, but in the dream too I still somehow knew that he was dead. I would ask him how he was here – I was undoubtedly exploring his absence, but his new presence too. There was a lot of crying during this time – crying going to sleep and crying on waking up during the night. I found it an ease to be able to cry in the peace and quiet of my own bedroom. It softened the pain. I find grief is a bit like the Inniscarra dam where water has to be released to ease the pressure.

I suffered big bouts of 'if only'. If only I had been kinder to him! If only I had not always taken his kindness for granted! If only I had been a better listener! These thoughts constantly ran through me and almost strangled me with regrets.

Because Gabriel had been big-hearted and generous, I had always taken his goodness for granted. He was far less selfish than I am and in our marriage he had been the giver and I the taker. Now I whipped myself with regrets.

Then one day while out for tea with a friend, I picked up a table napkin of a scene with pheasants. I love pheasants. Later I rang Lena asking her to bring home a large canvas from the Cork Art Shop. Early the following morning I began painting, and I painted all day; it was a cold day in early January and it passed in a haze of turpentine and paint. That painting brought the first release from mental misery. It was too cold to garden, I could not write and I could not motivate myself to do anything in the house. But I could paint. What a blessing that was! It was a big canvas and kept me occupied for days. I would not say that I ended up with a great painting, but that didn't matter. It had made those cold, January days more bearable.

At the end of January the marmalade oranges came into the shops. Now, I am a marmalade maker, but that year I had to kick myself into bringing home the oranges and making a start. Ellen and I prepared the oranges and as the smell of marmalade-making filled the kitchen I felt an easing of the knot of pain that is grief. The journey through bereavement is made up of tiny steps. Creativity is one of them.

With the first breath of spring I took to the garden. The earth is the greatest healer of all. There is something in the earth that soaks into the bloodstream and eases the mind. After hours of digging I would always feel better. There is no logic to this, but it works. Then I decided to redesign the garden and spent days digging up the lawns and converting them into flower beds interlaced with stone paths. It was back-breaking, tiring work, but had the blessing that I fell into bed exhausted every night. Despite this I still woke in the early hours and watched the grey light of dawn creep in the widow. Then I would put on soothing tapes and CDs and listen again and again to John O'Donoghue's voice. I scratched for climbing steps wherever I could find them in the hard wall of grief. It's what we must do and somehow when we search, those steps are there.

Climbing

I claw up

The black rock

Face of grief

With grim determination

Seeking tiny footholds

Gripping each ledge

Because if I should slip

I fall into nothingness

But if I keep climbing
You will be there
In the sunshine
Of wholeness.

Cold Dawn

Grey light seeps in
And the razor edge
Of realisation cuts
Through my waking mind.
The coldness of aloneness
Chills my nakedness

Have I the courage
To reinvent myself
Because I was part
Of a whole?

My first time doing anything on my own was a huge battle
and sometimes I would wonder if it was worth the effort.

The Back Yard

Yesterday I washed the back yard
With a mind full of throbbing pain.
Scalding tears joined piped water
Through hoses that you connected.

It is in the ordinary everyday
That I miss you most.
When all was clean and rearranged
I asked myself, 'Why did I bother?'

But you were never one
To sit and moan;
You would have kept going,
And so must I.

Because savage grief
Must be worked through
And grappled with hour by hour
So that one day your memory
Becomes a glorious tub of flowers.

Going places on my own for the first time was a bleak experience.

The Gap

We had gone
There together
Now I went alone
And could not fill the space;
Wanted to go home,
To lock myself in
Where I did not
Have to hold back tears
And pretend to be normal.

A Little Healing

'Come to Writers' Week
It might help a little.'
I doubted it!

There we created
Fantasy worlds
And I left reality behind.
When I came home
A little healing
Had happened.

Chapter 8

Morning Has Broken

She was a real home bird who should not have flown far from the nest. Ellen never quite transplanted her roots from Ireland to her adoptive country, Canada, and initially came home every summer. As she had married a Canadian who was an only child, there was no extended Canadian family and her children, especially her only daughter, Kelly, grew up very close to her Irish cousins who regarded her as part of all our families. So it was no surprise when, after many years flying back and forth, Ellen decided to over-winter in Ireland and avoid the harsh Canadian snows. She spent her summers in Toronto and in the autumn came to Innishannon, returning in the spring to Canada. We joked that she was a swallow in reverse.

I was always glad to be one of five sisters because there is great companionship in sisters. When we were all young there was a close bond between us, but over the years as we all went our separate ways and got involved in our own families, naturally that bond eased, but when Ellen came back to Innishannon we fell straight back into the old pattern. It was like picking up the needles on a piece of knitting that you had put down a long time ago, but the stitches were still on the needles and your found your way back into the old pattern with ease. We enjoyed the same kind of books, the same TV programmes and could spend hours chatting about all kinds of everything. She had a consuming interest in politics – local, national and worldwide – and kept up to date on political agendas all over the globe. Gardening and art were shared passions and we spent hours in our upstairs studio painting and monitoring each other's progress.

When she came to live in Innishannon she became involved in the life of the village and enjoyed all the local activities. She was always fascinated by the intricacies of living in a small community and would sometimes say in bemusement, 'I don't know if I would ever have survived in a small village.' Nevertheless, she was often astonished at the lengths the people of a small community would go to in support of each other or a local cause and often remarked, 'The people of Innishannon are amazing.'

But of all the occasions we shared, her greatest source

of pleasure was the annual Rossmore Drama Festival every March which we attended nightly for ten nights. The cream of Irish amateur drama graced the stage of this little theatre in the depths of West Cork and she marvelled at the amazingly high standard of the productions of plays from the pens of the best of Irish and international writers. She got to know the other theatre goers who shared her passion, in particular Noreen and Michael who always sat in front of us – and at the interval the four of us adjudicated the play ahead of the real adjudicator who came on stage at the end of the performance. Rossmore was the highlight of Ellen's year.

She walked with me along the grief road when time stood still for me after the deaths of our good friend, Con, and my husband, Gabriel. I was so lucky to have her. Kind and gentle by nature, she was a calming presence and a listening ear, and while I dug my grief into the garden behind the house she cooked in the kitchen and prepared great meals. I cook only when I get hungry, but Ellen loved pottering around the kitchen and trying out new recipes just for the fun of it. We were the ideal house-sharing combination, with me as gardener-cum-housekeeper and she as cook and comforter.

Every spring when we waved her off at Shannon airport we looked forward to her return in the autumn. One year after her daughter Kelly's wedding, which we all attended in Toronto, her Canadian family all came back to Innishannon for an Irish reception. We had spent weeks getting the house and garden ready for the big event and had enjoyed the whole thing immensely. After the wedding celebrations Ellen went back to Toronto, planning to return for Christmas. It was not to be.

Just before Christmas she was diagnosed with terminal cancer and on Christmas Eve Lena and I flew to Canada to spend Christmas with her. I had never spent Christmas anywhere other than at home and if anybody had asked me where I would least like to be on Christmas Eve I would have said Heathrow airport. But there we were, late on Christmas Eve on our way to a snow-covered Canada. It was great to see Ellen and Kelly and the rest of the family. She looked well and was in good spirits, but, being a nurse, she had no illusions about what lay ahead for her.

On Christmas morning we walked down the road to Mass in the local church, treading our way carefully along the ice- and snow-encrusted street. The houses along the way were festooned with dancing Santas and prancing reindeers. The Mass was leisurely and celebratory – we Irish must be the only crowd who get out our stop-watch and put a time limit on Mass! We found the slow pace of that Mass comforting because deep in all our hearts that morning we knew that this was the world from where we would need to draw strength in the months ahead.

That evening Lena, Kelly, and her husband, Rick, joined a family gathering in the home of Rick's sister, leaving Ellen and me to share a quiet meal in her lovely home looking out over a snow-covered city. It was a peaceful time together. Then Kelly, knowing that I love ballet, had booked tickets for *The Nutcracker* the following evening. It was enchanting – the exquisite beauty of the performance swept us into the translucent world of make-believe. We all came home feeling that we had been transported to a glorious realm. In the headlights of approaching sadness your sensory perception is finely tuned.

Lena and I came back to Ireland hoping that the planned treatment would bring extended time for Ellen and at the beginning things went fairly well, but on subsequent visits to Toronto through the year I witnessed her become more and more frail. On one occasion she met me at the airport in a soft pale-blue coat and I felt she looked like a piece of delicate china. Just before Christmas my sister, Theresa, and I decided to go over longterm and help take care of her with her wonderful daughter, who was now pregnant with her first baby. But there was to be no longterm as she died quietly a few days after we got there.

Later that night I went down into her basement apartment and there on the side of the fridge was a smiling picture of my beloved sister with Noreen and Michael, taken the previous year at Rossmore Drama Festival where she had spent so many great nights. It was hard to absorb the fact that she would never again enjoy Rossmore.

Ellen had always said that she wanted to be cremated, considering it far more hygienic than the alternative. The day after her death, Kelly and Rick held a reception for her in their house, where their friends and Ellen's gathered; it was in many ways similar to an Irish wake. On the morning of the actual cremation it was necessary for a family member to visit the crematorium, so Rick and I drove there. She looked so peaceful and totally natural, wrapped in a white sheet in a simple wooden box. Just as she would have wished. In beside her I slipped our mother's well-worn rosary beads in its little crumpled leather purse and a small bottle of holy water. She had never liked fuss and wanted only simplicity in life. This was as simple as it could be. The following day her ashes, in her favourite wooden box, stood in front of the altar at Mass and we sang her favourite hymn 'Morning Has Broken'.

With her baby due in two months, Kelly was unable to travel to Ireland but wanted her mother's ashes brought back to Innishannon. I could not bear the idea of Ellen's ashes being booked in with the luggage on the plane, but wished to take them on board with me. This was possible as I had a laptop which I put in with my luggage and put the ashes into my laptop bag which I carried on board over my shoulder. I felt much better being able to do this and the crematorium had provided all the necessary documentation. The airport authorities in both Pearson in Toronto and Schiphol in Amsterdam were helpful and courteous, and displayed an amazing amount of consideration and sensitivity. It restored my faith in the goodness of human nature and made me appreciate that not all officialdom is run by robots and we are not entirely hidebound by beaurocracy.

Theresa's daughter, Eileen, met us at Cork airport but arriving back in Innishannon was not easy. Eileen's husband, Paddy, who is a wood turner, had made a beautiful elm box for the ashes, so we placed it on a little table in the *seomra ciúin*, surrounded with lit candles in Aunty Peg's brass candlesticks. That night the family gathered for the rosary and it was particularly peaceful in the following days to be able to sit there in the quietness of the house where Ellen and I had spent so many happy hours together. Some of her close friends called and we had tea by the fire and chatted. It was a quiet and spiritual time, spent in the presence of someone who had never liked big crowds and fuss.

We did not put a death notice in the paper as all those who meant most to her were aware of her death and so her funeral was just family and very close friends. She never liked our big funerals and told me once that Irish funerals were like a war. So she did not have a 'war', but like the gentle lady that she was, she had a gentle homecoming. Paddy and I had dug her grave which was not a big undertaking with only ashes involved. On a little table beside it we placed a beautiful blue silk shawl belonging to my daughter, Lena, and after the funeral Mass we placed the little elm box on it. When the prayers were said we sang 'Morning Has Broken' and then eased the blue shawl containing the elm box down into the earth beside Gabriel, Uncle Jacky and Aunty Peg.

Two months later her first grandchild was born in Toronto and when she was five months old, Kelly and Rick brought her back to Innishannon to be christened. Fr Denis did the christening and after the beautiful church ceremony we walked down to Ellen's grave where Denis used the same holy water to bless her grandmother's resting place. The sun shone as we sang.

Morning Has Broken

Morning has broken, like the first morning
Blackbird has spoken, like the first bird
Praise for the singing, praise for the morning
Praise for them springing fresh from the Word.

Sweet the rain's new fall, sunlit from heaven
Like the first dewfall, on the first grass
Praise for the sweetness of the wet garden
Sprung in completeness where His feet pass.

Mine is the sunlight, mine is the morning
Born of the one light, Eden saw play
Praise with elation, praise every morning
God's resurrection of the new day.

The Shelter
Belt

Chapter 9

Of Hilly Places

Our Uncle Danny did not choose his words carefully and he had a raw honesty that could sometimes make life uncomfortable, especially if you decided to outwit him in an argument – he was lucky to have lived before political correctness became the order of the day. For many years he was a bachelor farmer, living with my grandmother. You could never describe him as a measured man: he had a great heart, a volatile temper and a huge sense of occasion. He and my grandmother ran the farm and because they were both determined people there was often a resounding clash of wills. He was my mother's only brother and where she was quiet and diplomatic, he was forthright and dogmatic.

When we were dispatched as children back the road to

help my grandmother, who was a strict disciplinarian, he would help to brighten up the visit with his entertaining stories; we were usually regaled with these stories as we all sat around the table at dinner time. Uncle Danny took his place at the head of the table and he did not tell his stories quietly, but acted them out in a loud voice, sometimes pounding the table for dramatic impact. When he did this the cutlery and cups bounced off the old wooden table, and I held my breath because sometimes some of them bounced with a clatter onto the stone floor! He was a dramatist at heart and in us he had a receptive audience. His version of 'Grace after Meals' was: 'I pray to the Almighty God that this feed may do me great good and that I might sleep sound tonight.'

Sometimes his colourful, descriptive phrases brought a frown to my grandmother's face, but I loved them because what they lacked in delicacy they made up for in clarity. One day he was telling us about a woman whom he had met in town and who had insisted in telling him a long-winded story about her operation, in which he had no interest. He explained that he had tried to cut her short and move on, but had not succeeded. This to me was difficult to understand, because as far as I was concerned it would be difficult to stop Uncle Danny in his tracks.

So I questioned him: 'But why couldn't you get rid of her?'

'Because I'll tell you why,' he asserted, pounding the table in vexation, 'she was like a waxy hen's shit' – and two knives hit the floor.

He put me on my first pony and terrified the living daylights out of me. The pony was in the yard after coming home from the creamery, still with some of her harness on. I was eyeing her, wondering about getting up on her back, when Uncle Danny took hold of me and unceremoniously swung me up there – and the surprised pony took off, with me clinging onto her loose harness that soon parted company with the pony and slid to the ground, bringing me with it in a tangle of leather straps and chains. I didn't speak to him for the rest of the day, but the following morning when he went to the creamery he brought back a peace offering of a big brown paper bag of sweets.

As far as Uncle Danny was concerned, *his* cattle dog was smarter than any other dog in the parish. He was also into greyhounds, and *his* greyhounds were the best and the fastest, and he could spend hours expounding on their virtues; even if they were beaten at the racetrack it was never their fault, it was always 'the Bon Secours bend' that was their undoing – that was the bend in the track next to the hospital run by the Bon Secours nuns and was blamed for many a failure at the Cork track! In Uncle Danny's world, everything was always going to turn out great.

He always wore a big, wide-brimmed cowboy hat. At the time, emigration to Oregon to herd cattle for out-of-work young lads or those with wanderlust in their blood was part of our culture, and years later they all came home on holiday sporting what we called Oregon-man's hats. Uncle Danny had never been to Oregon, but he took a fancy to the hat – and it suited his personality, and he sometimes used it to open and close a conversation. Often having said his 'Grace after Meals' he would don his hat with a flourish and burst into song as he walked out into the farmyard, his dogs dancing with delight around him while he sang at the top of his voice:

'I'm sailing along in a trolly,
I feel like a big millionaire . . . '

When the time for cutting the hay came around he emerged from the haggard perched up on the mowing machine and guiding his two horses like Ben Hur charging a chariot through ancient Rome. Sometimes in the winter, as we lived in the hills along the Cork–Kerry border, we got very heavy snowfalls and could be snowed in for long periods. Then Uncle Danny would arrive at our farm on horseback, bringing supplies and checking that everything was in order. He was larger than life and seemed to come into his own in difficult circumstances.

My grandmother and he often locked horns. If he went to a cattle fair or pig market and decided to go to the pub afterwards with his friends, then came home later feeling merry, there was a right royal battle. My grandmother lambasted him with a tirade of caustic comments, but he did not let her get away with it and held his own in a shower of elaborate retorts. I think he enjoyed this verbal warfare, but occasionally, when my grandmother decided to 'take to the bed', it confounded and irritated him intensely. He would come down to our house and tell my mother, in an aggrieved tone of voice, that 'Herself has a touch of Oliver.' He always referred to my grandmother as 'Herself' or 'The Missus'. We called her Nana Ballyduane. He could deal with her when she stood her ground and confronted him, but when she decided that she was not long for this world and took to her bed, even though he knew that she was pulling a stunt, he would not call her bluff. He knew and we knew that there was really nothing wrong with her, but at the same time she was well on in years and there was always the possibility that she could be calling it a day. But she always rose again and 'Oliver', whatever or whoever he was, disappeared until the next time.

Each of us in turn served our time at my grandmother's house as my mother would play the guilt card of sending us back the road 'to help poor Nana'. My grandmother was a very unsuitable candidate for such a description as she was a tall, able-bodied woman, who was into herbal cures – even for the animals she rarely summoned a vet as she believed that she knew far more than most of them and boasted that she had never lost a sick animal. She was widowed early in life and ran the farm with great efficiency and was in absolute control until Danny grew up and took her on.

When we were adults and left home we always visited the two of them when we were back for weekends or on holiday and Uncle Danny would be very disappointed if he was out when we called. Once he was not at home when I visited and early the following morning he appeared before breakfast at our house having detoured on his way to the creamery. When I protested about this inconvenience to him, I was told in no uncertain fashion: 'These are the things that are important in life, Aliceen,' (he always called me that) 'keeping in touch and supporting each other, that's what family is all about. Don't you ever forget that!'

In later years he got married and was blessed that he found a wife who not only understood him, but adored the ground that he walked on. Ours is a long-tailed family and she kept an open door for all of us and once, in later years, when paying an unplanned visit I found them with their three children around the same table and he still holding forth and they, like us, delighted with his performance. I left the house thinking what a lucky man he was.

But his luck was about to run out. One day my mother rang to say that he had gone into hospital. My initial reaction was one of dismay. How could this larger-than-life country man, who had never been to a doctor in his life, cope with the constraints of a hospital? My initial dismay turned to anguish when I saw him – he was tied and bound by wires and tubes to the narrow hospital bed. A scene from his farm flashed into my mind: each year at the start of winter he would bring into the stalls the heifers who had spent their early life in the fields along by the river. They had never known restraint, but now because winter was here they had to be brought in to shelter from the winter cold. They were terrified and when they were finally tied into their stalls, their eyes dilated in fear. They had only known freedom. He too had only known freedom and was now imprisoned. My heart bled for him. After many months of suffering, death came as a blessed release and I prayed that wherever he went there were open fields and hilly places where he could wear his big Oregon-man's hat.

Uncle Danny

He was a man
Who took life
By the throat
And demanded what was his.
Moderation was not his theme,
Rather, excess in all things,
Even in the greatness
Of his heart.

And Time Stood Still

You could forgive him
Many faults
Because of so great a heart.
He lived life
With the spontaneity
Of a rushing river
That could not be blocked;
And yet it was stopped short
In full flood.
My heart ached to see him
Tubed by nose and hand,
Strapped like a wild creature
In his hospital bed;
A frightened animal,
Unaccustomed to restraint,
Brought in to shelter
From the winter cold,
Eyes dilated in terror.
A man of hilly places
Trapped in antiseptic crucifixion;
Slow death dragged on for months,
This mighty man withered.
The torrent
Declined to a trickle
And then was no more.

Chapter 10

One of Us

He was my first brother-in-law. As I was the youngest of five sisters it was very important to me that he would prove a positive addition to the family – this brother-in-law, with the possibility of three more to follow, could be an indication of things to come! He came into our lives when he married our sister, Theresa. I was a teenager at the time, so he came in for a fair bit of scrutiny as teenagers can be merciless and judgemental. But he passed all tests with flying colours.

They lived in the nearby town which was a big plus as it meant that we now had a base from where we could go dancing and to the local cinema. Their door was always open to us and Bill welcomed us with warm approval. Our sister could be strict, but Bill always poured oil on troubled waters and provided a free taxi service for us as well. As far as I was concerned, he was a great extension to the family.

When the extension stretched to three little nieces I became a not very efficient babysitter as I had no knowledge of babies – but they survived my inexperience. Later, two boys joined the family and every Sunday they piled into their Volkswagen Beetle and came back to the home farm. As they grew up, we were always in close contact and when I got married and ran a guest house the girls became my summer-holiday workforce. They were reliable and cheerful, and we survived many hurdles together. Having done a course at the cookery school in Ballymaloe, two of them decided to open their own confectionery business. So they moved in next door to our old house that was now empty as we had moved into part of the guest house – it was a big step for two young girls but after a lot of discussion the decision was finally reached. Then their father told them, 'Wrong or right, you are right now anyway' – he always advised that once a decision was made, that was it! He was a great encourager and one of his philosophies was: it's a good thing to know when you are well off. Bill was kind and easygoing, and we all loved him.

When a thunderbolt comes out of the blue, you always remember afterwards exactly where you were when it struck; it is as if shock imprints the surroundings on the mind. On a beautiful sunny June evening in 1980 I was pottering around the kitchen. My husband, Gabriel, was at a match and my cousin, Con, who lived with us, was sitting by the Aga reading a book. The phone out in the hallway rang and I strolled out to answer it. I picked it up casually, thinking that it was one of my sisters. The doctor from my home place was on the line, which immediately put me on red alert. At first I could not take in what he was saying, so I gasped, 'Say that again.'

'Bill Allen has just died,' he told me.

'Are you sure?' I demanded.

'Alice, I'm a doctor and I know when someone is dead,' he assured me gently.

'But how?' I gasped

'A heart attack,' he said, and continued slowly and firmly as if he knew that I was not taking things in. 'I'm here with Theresa. There are others here. So don't rush. Bring the girls. Take your time.'

'But when did it happen?' I was still grasping at straws, hoping that in some way he had got it wrong and it was not true.

'Just now. They came home from a match and were having their tea and he died very suddenly.'

I put down the phone and stood rooted to the floor. How was I going to tell the girls? I went back into the kitchen and blurted out the news to Con.

'How am I going to tell the girls?' I demanded.

'You'll just have to,' he told me quietly, 'there's no one else to do it.'

I walked around the kitchen to get my thinking sorted and trying to figure out the best way to do it. But I could not think. My mind had gone numb. I just walked blindly around and around the table, trying to absorb what I had just been told. Finally, I went slowly along the corridor and stood outside their door. I could hear them laughing inside. I knew that once I went in that door they would not laugh for a long time. I really did not want to go in and say it – in my confused mind I felt that if it was not said, it was as if it had not happened, but once said, like cracking ice, the whole world around them would fall asunder. But it had to be done. I gripped the knob and slowly opened the door. They turned two welcoming faces towards me and I recall that Mary held a mug with red roses on it in her hand.

'We're just making tea,' she told me, smiling, and then seeing my face her smile faded. 'What's wrong?' Sensing her alarm, Eileen immediately swung around. They knew instantly that I had terrible news. There was no way to cushion this shock. We sat down and I told them as gently as I could the news that you could not make gentle. They looked at me with disbelieving faces, their world crashing around them. The beloved father, who had sustained and encouraged them all their lives, was dead. It was almost too much to take in. They sat in stunned silence, too shattered to think. Then we cried and talked for a long time as they tried to absorb what had happened. Finally it was a case of jerking back into the reality of thinking about what had to be done.

Their sister, Treasa, who was teaching in Clonakilty, had to be told. By then Gabriel was home, and he and Con went west to break the news to her that would change all their lives.

Later that night we drove through the quiet countryside of Macroom, Carriganimma and finally their home place in Newmarket. Eileen later told me that she felt that if we just kept on driving and never arrived it might be that this terrible thing had never occurred. Their father was laid out in the front room, almost as if he was asleep. Trying to absorb the enormity of his death was mind-boggling for them, but his presence there made it all real. For the first time I realised the value of a home wake. This mourning time was necessary. If the girls had come home and his body had been whipped away to a funeral parlour, it would all have been much harder for them to take in. But they had that whole night and the following day to be with him in his death. Though it was terrible, it was necessary for their minds to have the time to absorb the reality. It was difficult to know how much their little eight-year-old brother was taking in.

Some time during that day I went with my sister, Phil, to tell our parents, who were both still alive then. Bill had been their first son-in-law and had become a second son to them. They took it with grace and I learned of the resilience and the fortitude of that generation. During their lives they had seen death many times.

The removal to the church and the funeral passed in a fog and Theresa coped on the auto-pilot reaction that is part of every sudden death. Later that night she surprised me by saying quietly, 'I missed George from the funeral. How come he wasn't there? We were always such friends.' I was amazed that amongst the crowds who attended she could miss just one person – in the midst of trauma there is still a part of us that is absorbing facts. It is then we need the support of special friends. A wonderful letter given to her by a close friend of Bill's brought her comfort. Friendship is one of the handrails that keep us standing when the ground shakes beneath us.

During the following months Theresa walked the grief road and years afterwards she told me that she would, in the months after his death, sometimes drive to Muckross Park in Killarney, a place that she and Bill had often visited together, and she would sit on a bench there for long periods and look at the trees – and would not have been surprised if Bill had walked out of them and sat with her. The reality of a sudden death takes a long time to absorb and the reshaping of a new world is a slow journey. During those months I wrote the following poem but never gave it to her.

Theresa's Journey

Your suffering was terrible to see
We suffered for you
But we were in an outer circle,
No one could reach inside
The torture chamber of your mind.
Your gaping wound could not be touched
It had to be licked clean by you,
Like a wounded animal in its lair
You lay bleeding for many months.
Then numbness gone
You crawled forward
Into a darker tunnel,
But this at least led out
From your lonely lair.
Now you prayed
And cried to heaven for mercy,
But we could not lead you
From this place.
An inner strength
Born of a greater power
Could only bring you through.
And then it came to help you
And so you stumbled on

Gaining strength from a source
Greater than your sorrow.
And on the day you smiled
You first real smile,
We thanked God
That with his help
Burdens can be borne.

Looking back now with the wisdom of hindsight I realise that during that time I was of very little help to Theresa. Because I had yet to experience the devastation of grief as an adult I had no idea how necessary it was to be in constant touch with her. I realise now that in the void of the months, and indeed the years after a death, people need the nurture and support of family, friends and neighbours. This can be given by keeping in regular contact and through constant little acts of kindness. These are the stepping stones that lead people to an easier place.

During the month following their father's death the girls were with us in Innishannon so we were able to sit and talk for long periods. During that time I wrote a poem for them and thirty years afterwards, in 2010 when I began to write this book, Mary gave it back to me. I had forgotten it, but she had kept it all those years because it had brought her comfort.

Bill

Never created any fuss
We loved this man
Who was one of us.
He married our sister
And became our friend
Because on him
We could depend.
Always welcome
To come and stay
Warmed by his placid way.
Guided their children
By a constant light
He did not preach
But showed them right.
Tess and he rowed
A steady boat
She packed the cargo
He steadied the load.
When he came to
Waters quiet
He anchored home
On a summer's night.
His going reflected
An approach to life
Gentle and calm
Without stress or strife.

And Time Stood Still

On that warm June day
Each remembered
His kindly way
Sunshine and singing
Warmed our tears
Recalling memories
Of happy years.
In Clonfert 'neath
A patch of green
On a simple stone
Can his name be seen.
A loving husband
Father and friend
A gentle man
To the very end.

Chapter 11

The Gardener

When I married Gabriel and went to live in Innishannon my mother's advice was, 'You are now going to be part of another family and don't you be the cause of any trouble.' At the time I didn't know what she was talking about. As it happened, my new husband's parents were both dead and he had been reared by his Aunty Peg and Uncle Jacky, who both thought that he had three halos! Aunty Peg viewed me as a potential problem – and she was right because, like two stones in a bucket, she and I rubbed off each other until I got my corners rounded. But Uncle Jacky was an all-forgiving, wonderful man, whom I loved dearly from day one. Maybe he and Peg were a good combination because she never let anybody get away with

anything, whereas Jacky only saw what was good in everyone, which could be a risky business if you were running
the village shop and all your customers had little red account
books and very few dealt in cash!

Jacky was a great gardener and, of course, he dished out his
garden produce free of charge across the counter. He worked
on the principle that it had cost him nothing and he never
counted the price of his gardening because to him it was a
pure labour of love. It was his time off from the shop and was
his all-consuming passion.

Aunty Peg, however, worked on a different principle. She
made jams and jellies from his gooseberries, raspberries and
blackcurrants and charged what she considered her due for
it, though if she liked you there could be an extra pot slipped
into your message bag! I learned a lot from the pair of them.
They knew everybody in the parish and could trace their
family roots back for generations. If you wanted an edited
version, you asked Uncle Jacky, who told you all the good
things about all his relations, but if you wanted the full, una-
bridged edition, you asked Aunty Peg.

Jacky was a saint and his garden was his heaven. I loved
his garden – the first time I saw it I thought that I had ram-
bled into the pages of a children's book. It sloped up from
the back door and right at the top, at the end of a winding
path, was the henhouse. He had built this himself under the
trees in the grove, as well as all the other little rickety sheds

around the garden that were used for his tools, and his cats and dogs. The hens – Rhode Island Reds, Wyandottes and Sussex – had the run of the garden where they scratched between drills of potatoes, rhubarb and onions. The hens were like the league of nations and we enjoyed a great mix of eggs: large and small, white and brown. Jacky was not into pruning, so there was a flowing abundance about that entire garden – his rambling roses climbed over homemade wooden arches and across nearby hedges. Almost everything that he grew found its way onto the kitchen table and visitors never went home empty-handed. As a young man he had planted apple trees and crab-apple trees so Aunty Peg was never short of supplies for making what in later years became known in our family as 'Aunty Peg's Apple Cake'. At Christmas his holly trees decorated not only our house, but many other village houses too. It made me realise the wisdom of having your own holly trees as you didn't have to go scrambling across wet fields on cold winter days, and every year I bless him at Christmas when I can just go out the back door and cut his holly.

Jacky's gardening was all about enjoyment. No matter what he was doing, when you went out to see him in the garden he had time to lean on his spade and have a chat, and he loved to walk you around and explain things to you. He would make anyone love gardening because he exuded such a sense of pleasure in it. In his shop he was fast-moving and efficient, but it was as if he took off that coat when he came out into his garden and here his true spirit emerged. He relaxed and glowed with contentment. Sometimes, if you came on him unawares, he would have his rosary beads twined around his fingers, as he weeded and prayed. Our children loved him and he thought that they were perfect which, of course, led to a mutual adoration society. He never saw any wrong in them, which meant that they got away with murder! Every second week he took them on the bus to Bandon to get their hair cut, and they always got more than a haircut!

But Jacky did not confine his goodness to his home, shop and garden. Every morning he ran around the village and delivered the paper to all the houses on his way to daily Mass, and also delivered milk and the paper to the priest, changed the bulbs in the church when needed and cut the grass in the graveyard. He was a maintenance man for the entire village. But if someone overstepped the mark and took advantage of his goodness, Aunty Peg intervened and sorted them out in no uncertain fashion. As time went on, I grew to appreciate Aunty Peg's stalwart qualities and I would sometimes remember my mother's description of my grandmother: she'd kill you and she'd cure you.

Jacky's other great love was the GAA. He had played, refereed and held every club officership in his local and divisional club. The most valuable piece of jewellery that I now possess is a gold medal that he got from his local West Cork GAA division, dated with his terms of office 1924-1927, and Aunty Peg had it fashioned it into a beautiful broach. Because of its history it is deeply treasured.

Whereas Aunty Peg, who was a woman of some size and stature, occasionally felt the need of medical aid, Jacky was slim and athletic and as fit as a fiddle, and never bothered any doctor. So when, in the small hours of a cold November morning in 1977, he got a heart attack, it came as a bolt from the blue. Aunty Peg arrived at the foot of our stairs calling for help, and Gabriel and I tumbled downstairs, ran through the adjoining shop and up their stairs, where Jacky was sitting up in bed, ashen-faced. Dr Cormac, who lived down the road, was there within minutes and then Gabriel and Jacky were on the road to the hospital in Cork. He recovered, but there was a long, hard road ahead of him and he spent months in hospital, during which time as a result of complications he had to have a leg amputated.

Gabriel and I visited every night and he was an amazing patient who always had a cheery word for everyone. On the night after his amputation operation I was apprehensive, fearing that he would be very upset, but rather than us comforting him it was he who made it easy for us. Finally, he came home with a crutch and a very positive attitude. His old friends and neighbours visited him and on warm, sunny days he sat in his beloved garden. But it was a tough time for him because this active man, who had spent his life looking after others now was in the reverse situation. He found his artifical limb cumbersome and difficult to manage, and so the next step was the rehabilitation centre in faraway Dun Laoghaire, outside Dublin, where he would be trained to use it.

On a bright sunny July day, Gabriel and I drove him up to Dun Laoghaire, but as we said goodbye to him at the hospital I could see for the first time a deep sadness in his eyes. Every day Aunty Peg and I wrote to him and posted on the *Cork Examiner* – we wanted to keep him in touch with the local news until he came home. But he never came home. Early one morning there was a phone call to say that during the night he had had a fatal heart attack.

Aunty Peg was devastated and Gabriel and I headed back up to Dun Laoghaire to bring Uncle Jacky home. I dreaded arriving there and seeing the body of this wonderful man whom we all loved so much. But the strange thing was that even in death he made it easy for us because on arrival we found ourselves looking at the smiling face of someone who was completely at peace.

On this occasion I was again reminded of small kindnesses that mean so much at such times: it was comforting to meet Innishannon people, now living in Dublin, who had come to be with us. Because of it, the journey home was an easier one and Jacky arrived into the village to be welcomed by a guard of honour of the GAA club that he had served so well.

Early on the morning of his funeral I walked up through his beloved garden where his roses were in full bloom. The birds were singing and white butterflies fluttered around his rambling roses. This had been his heaven on earth. I hoped that wherever Jacky was now he had a garden, because there he could create his own heaven. In his garden he left behind a wonderful heritage which, in subsequent years, became my own healing place when other bereavements came my way.

Jacky's Garden

Here there is no set layout,
Nature's freedom is all about.
A garden cared by loving hands,
Green profusion, nothing planned.

Flowers and fruit freely abound;
Bees in their hives hum a mellow sound;
No regimented hedges in orderly array:
This is a garden with nature's sway.

A haven created by a man of love,
Man of the earth, with thoughts of above;
Here nature, love and care combine
To create a refuge, an escape from time.

Chapter 12

A Woman of Substance

In the weeks following Jacky's death, Aunty Peg seemed to shrink. While she appeared to have been the strong one in the relationship, Jacky had actually supplied the fine threads that had held their world together. He had provided a deep, resilient pool in which Peg had the security to be totally at ease and to depend on him to provide silent support. With his going, that security was gone. Because she and I had lived for so long in such close proximity, I was aware of this and on the day of his funeral as I stood by Jacky's grave I found myself asking him how she was going to cope without him. This may sound a bit hard to believe, but in some way it filtered through my mind that Peg would soon follow after him. Even in death he was taking care of us. So when, within a few weeks, Dr Cormac referred her to hospital for tests it did not come as a complete surprise. She was diagnosed with cancer, and rather than accept treatment she discharged herself and came home declaring that she could not 'put up with all that carry-on' and that she wanted to die at home in her own bed.

At first I was a bit perplexed by this unorthodox approach, even though I should not have been surprised because Peg was always a law unto herself. Dr Cormac, who knew her well, was understanding of her decision, telling me, 'It's her choice and we will respect it.'

'But will we be able to cope?' I asked.

'We will cope,' he assured me. 'I'll be there when she needs me.' And he was true to his word.

For the first few months Peg was able to manage and pottered around her own little house and then her sister, Mary, always known as Min, came to stay with her. But that arrangement did not last long as they had never got on too well and after a few weeks sparks flew and Min abandoned ship and was on the bus back home to Cork. Peg was all right on her own during the day, with someone popping in and out, but she needed company at night. She had always been a bad sleeper and she now found the nights very long. With the departure of Min, one of our boys, Seán, slept in her room. He was ten years old, and at night they had long chats and he grew extremely fond of her – and during that time he learnt long prayers, the family history and all about the life of the parish!

After Jacky's funeral Peg had got a huge number of cards and letters from around the parish, and indeed from around the world, as Jacky had been a cornerstone in the village for so long. Now, every day after breakfast, she sat down at the table in her little sitting room and proceeded to answer all this correspondence, sometimes with long, detailed letters. She was a great letter writer. Her application to this task, despite all the trauma she was going through, was admirable and her letter writing in some way seemed to ease the pain of her grief. She may have found it difficult to articulate her feelings to those around her, so letters to old friends were a great outlet for expressing her hurt: the deep wound of grief needs expression to be healed.

Gradually her condition became more frail and she needed more care at night, so Seán and I switched places and I became her night nurse. After his amputation Jacky had slept downstairs, but Aunty Peg refused to leave her familiar bedroom and eventually she was unable to climb the stairs. Her bedroom became her sanctuary – indeed, her whole world – which she shared with her dog, Topsy, and myself. Topsy, in his day, had been a small, light little terrier but now, after years of over-loving, had grown into a big, soft, white ball, waddling around on four props and he could barely climb up the stairs – and sometimes had to air-lifted from the rear.

All her life Aunty Peg had been forthright and sometimes demanding, but now she became tolerant and gentle. Every night before going to sleep we both had a brandy and port because it helped her to sleep, and one night she told me, 'If I don't die soon you'll be an alcoholic!'

Regarding the matter of dying, I was never quite sure if she really wanted to know the details or not, because one day she would want to know and the next day she would be planning a trip and had forgotten all about dying. I discussed it with Dr Cormac.

'When she asks me "Am I dying?" what do I tell her?' I asked him.

'Well, there are two ways of looking at it,' he told me. 'The modern way is to tell a patient their situation out straight, but I'm not sure that's always the wisest decision because then you take away their hope. At the moment Peg has good days when she feels well – well enough to make plans – but once you have answered that question she will remember it on the good days and it will take the pleasure out of them. And Peg probably has it worked it out for herself, anyway, but working it out and articulating it are two different things. Once something is said it gets imprinted on the mind.'

To me that made a whole lot of sense. A few days later when a long-forgotten cousin came to visit, I discovered that Peg was quite aware that she was on her final journey. While he chatted with her I went downstairs to make tea to bring to her room for the two of them, but on my way up he passed me on his way down, muttering under his breath. She was sitting up in bed having dispatched him on his way. She had never really liked this man and was quite annoyed that he had come at all, but when he told her she was looking well that was a step too far and she dismissed him in no uncertain terms.

'I have only to look in the mirror,' she said scornfully. 'It tells the whole story. Does that fellow think I'm a fool?'

But mostly she enjoyed her visitors, especially if it was somebody that she really liked, and I soon realised that it is important that only good friends visit you when you are very sick and that visitors do not stay too long. I appreciated the good neighbours who popped in and out, especially those who would sit quietly with her. The people who were most helpful and understanding were the people who had nursed a family member at home. To quote my sister Ellen's favourite phrase, 'They had walked in the shoes.'

Gradually Aunty Peg grew weaker and needed somebody with her at all times. It was a balancing act between several people: Dr Cormac called every day and was a tremendous support; and working in the shop at the time we had a wonderful girl, Ann, who constantly ran up and down the stairs to Peg between customers to make sure that all was well. The back-up of friends made coping possible and acts of unexpected kindness kept us going. One night just before Christmas I came downstairs to find a box of delicious mince pies on the table. It did my heart good. The younger children in our family visited Aunty Peg regularly and had no problem doing so, but the two older ones were upset by her appearance and found it much more difficult. As I walked with Peg through her final days I sometimes got the strange feeling that when she went I too might go with her – it was a crazy notion, born of exhaustion and too many long hours in the sick room.

Towards the end she began to have visions. One day when I went into her room she asked, 'Did you meet her?'

'Who?' I asked in surprise.

'The woman in grey. She was sitting there on the bed and went out the door just before you came in. You should have met her.'

On another occasion she talked about Jacky being in the room. She could see him sitting at the end of the bed. It was a most extraordinary time when I felt that we were living between two worlds.

Then, early one morning, she went into a coma and our neighbour, Betsy, sat with me and helped to alleviate the discomfort that comes with a slow death. As Aunty Peg eased out of life, a profound stillness seeped into the room. It folded itself around her bed like a soft veil. I felt that I was standing at the edge of a deep mystery into which I had no vision.

She had gone into an awesome silence that was beyond the limits of my human mind.

Afterwards I walked down the stairs and into her little sitting room and looked at the things that she had so lovingly collected and polished all her life. She would never again touch any of them – and the absolute finality of death hit me. It had been a long, hard journey, but I was glad that we had walked it together. After the funeral we locked the front door of her house and I did not go in there for several months. It would have seemed like a violation immediately to begin dismantling her little corner of the world and all that she held dear. She was gone, but I had no wish to eradicate her essence. Healing time was needed.

During that time I had a strange recurring dream in which I was running up the stairs of her house and then opening the door into her room, but finding nothing there. I would wake up in a panic, falling into nothingness. But gradually the dream faded away.

Jacky and Peg's house was to become part of the extended shop, so one day we took all her furniture out into the back yard, treated it for woodworm and polished it before moving it into our house. She had died in March and it took all summer to clear out their old house; Gabriel's niece, Dolores, came every day to help. Uncle Jacky's family had lived in that house for four generations. Going through old letters and pictures is a slow process, but very worthwhile because it is healing to the spirit to take the time to let loved ones go gently. It can be a sad and tearful experience too, but in some way we are sending them lovingly on their way. Over the years Aunty Peg had collected lovely bits and pieces which she had treasured and now, out of respect for her and Jacky, we too treasure them. Family collectables are valuable on account of the years of loving care that have been showered on them, and when somebody dies I have found it healing to treat what they leave behind with loving respect.

Scaffolding

When I am gone
And you who
Go through my things
Are left to sort,
Look kindly on
What I leave behind:
Jugs, pictures, books
And my beloved garden.
Maybe nothing valuable
In worldly eyes
But these are
The remnants of a life
That was filled
With beautiful moments,

And these things
Were the scaffolding.
Take them gently now
And lay them
Where they will
Be best loved.

Chapter 13

A Restless Spirit

After her sister Peg's death, Aunty Min became a regular visitor to our home. I was never quite sure whether I was an inadequate host or if Min was a demanding visitor, but wherever the fault lay, our house never quite measured up to her expectations. Maybe it had something to do with the fact that a husband and teenage children had never disrupted her own lifestyle. She had always been totally independent, never experiencing the restrictions of family life.

At the time we had four teenage boys and Aunty Min had no reason to know that teenagers leave the human race once they enter that zone and return only when their parents have served a long term of endurance. She was under the illusion that she could transform them into paragons of virtue, an ambition that I had long since abandoned. She regularly informed me that they were bad-mannered, badly trained and badly behaved. I had no magic formula to change them, but Aunty Min was convinced that she had, which led to an ongoing clash of opinions between her and the young males jumping with teenage hormones. Even our little girl, who insisted on taking her favourite doll to visit Aunty Min's bedroom, was smartly evicted.

Aunty Min was a superb cook and every year, once the tourist season began, she would take up a position at a different hotel where she cooked incredible meals. Once established in the kitchen, and having made herself indispensable to the running of the hotel, she then proceeded to lock horns with the various managers. She was convinced that she knew more about the hotel business than any manager, which did not contribute to ideal industrial relations. The result was that at the end of the season she left in a blaze of recrimination, swearing never to return, and the exhausted management breathed a sigh of relief. The following year she moved into another hotel where the same saga re-enacted itself all over again, but because she was so good at her job she was always in demand.

Once she had retired from the hotel scene and began visiting us, she took over the kitchen, which suited me fine, but her belief that cooking was central to the wellbeing of the universe often brought her into conflict with our brood. As far as Aunty Min was concerned, once a meal was on the table it took precedence over all other activities – even All-Ireland finals! This was in a house where the GAA was a second religion and it sometimes caused mayhem. One year Gabriel and I had gone to Croke Park taking some of the younger ones and leaving the others at home with Con, who lived with us, and just as the game began Aunty Min promptly turned off the TV and insisted that her perfectly cooked meal must be savoured there and then! Con did his best to maintain peace, but that night we came home to a revolution – and Aunty Min, in protest, was on the bus back to Cork the following morning declaring us to be an unappreciative lot.

Even when she was in the full of her health she was a hypochondriac and this condition accelerated as the years went on. Her handbag was like a mobile pharmacy where pills she had exchanged with her friends and out-of-date medicines accumulated.

Eventually, Aunty Min came to stay permanently. No longer well enough to live alone in her house in Cork, she moved to Innishannon. Her doctor had told us that her heart was in very poor condition and she had other medical complications. At the beginning she reigned supreme in the kitchen, but slowly she deteriorated and withdrew to her bedroom. In order to keep a constant eye on her, we gave her a bedroom beside the kitchen. She hated being confined to bed, so I gave her a big brass bell that she could ring when she needed anything. And it rang non-stop! Poor Aunty Min had always been a restless spirit and now that she was stuck in one place she found it very restrictive, and, unlike Aunty Peg, she was not an easy patient. She felt the cold intensely and despite having an electric blanket and a heater on full-blast, she constantly wanted her hot-water bottle refilled with hotter water. One of the boys found his own solution and would come outside the door, hold the boiling-hot bottle for a few minutes, and then go back in pretending that he had refilled it! Some days, after hours of bell ringing, I would come into the kitchen and grasp the taps of the sink and tell myself: Alice, you had better laugh because if you don't you'll cry. On the shelf above the sink was a little verse called 'Don't Quit' and when I was at the end of my tether I would read it and somehow it always keep me going. Caring for an old person at home can be a test of endurance and the only people who think that it is no bother are those who never did it!

Then, quite suddenly, it all came to an abrupt end. Going into her room late one Good Friday evening I sensed a sudden change: a certain quietness had descended. There was no more bell ringing and that night we sat up with her while she slowly went into a coma. Early on Easter Sunday morning she slipped quietly away. Her restless spirit was at last at peace.

Now at family celebrations I remember Aunty Min. As a wedding present she gave us a cream-coloured gilt-edged

dinner service, comprising numerous plates, serving bowls and casserole dishes, and when the extended family gathers together for special occasions, out comes Aunty Min's dinner service. As the creation of beautiful meals was one of the few things that brought joy to her life, it is fitting that she who loved food should be remembered at the table. Thank you, Aunty Min!

The
Unexpected

Chapter 14

The Motivator

The man with the violin edged his way unobtrusively through the mourners until he reached the foot of Steve's coffin. There he slowly eased the violin from under his arm, lifted the bow and a gentle wave of haunting notes enshrouded Steve and cast a silencing veil over the entire gathering. Steve McDonagh, who had founded Brandon Books and driven it on with vision and enthusiasm, had been suddenly whisked out of all our lives. We had gathered to say farewell.

There were no reverends in black albs and white surplices, and Steve did not seem to belong in these confined quarters. But the gentle notes of the violinist opened gates into fields of unploughed spirituality and this beautiful requiem bore the spirit of Steve above and beyond the edges of our human limitations. The music encompassed liturgy, prayers and ritual, a fitting swan-song for a man who had always reached above and beyond the mundane procedures of the expected.

Later that evening as my daughter, Lena, and I drove home through the gathering dusk between the beautiful Kerry mountains where Steve had chosen to live and set up Brandon Books, I thought back over the many years that we had worked together.

Twenty-four years earlier, in the spring of 1987, I had sent him the manuscript of *To School through the Fields*. I had assumed because of the name Brandon, and as it was based in Kerry, that I would be dealing with a Kerryman. But after the first two sentences on the phone with Steve I knew that this was no Kerryman; he sounded more like some unusual Irish-English mix. During that first conversation, I wondered how come he was running a publishing business from the depths of Dingle. I was to discover that he had immersed himself in the heritage and traditions of Dingle, especially the annual Wren Day, which was the highlight of his year.

As a result of his phone call we arranged to meet for lunch the following day. I encountered an affable, bearded, six-footer, and he subsequently told me that he had been expecting a shawled Peig Sayers! At the time I was probably lacking a few years and stiff limbs to fit that picture, but I am catching up fast!

On that day it was obvious that he was pleased with my manuscript and I came home on winged feet because having your first manuscript accepted by a publisher is a heady experience. Steve had given me instructions for more detail and extra chapters. This posed no problem and so during that summer, when the demands of work and a busy household had been attended to, I would sneak up to the attic and carry out his instructions. I posted the manuscript back to him in the autumn.

The publishing of *To School* set us on a journey and over the following years Brandon published fifteen more of my books. Steve was a merciless and superb editor. I got away with nothing. His constant refrain was, 'Do not part with your manuscript until you are completely satisfied and it is as good as it can be.' Pursuit of excellence was his goal and Steve would hack my material back to the bone and the result would sometimes lead to a mini war between us! During one of these conflicts I sent him a poem entitled 'The Verbal Butcher', which caused him great amusement.

I enjoyed working with Steve, and over the years writing and publishing with Brandon never lost its sense of challenge and enjoyment. Steve *was* Brandon. He edited, published and did the publicity. On one of his first visits to our house, he dragged Gabriel and myself out into the garden to take a photograph. My garden at the time was an overgrown wilderness, complete with goalposts and dogs. Steve looked around in dismay and enquired acidly, 'Is there any corner here that looks like a *garden*?' Many books and years later when I had caught the gardening bug, he stood and surveyed the now transformed garden and informed me, 'When I came here first it was all about writing and no gardening, now it's all gardening and no writing!'

But a visit from Steve would always change that and when he left after a day of tea and chat I was hooked on another project. He was a wonderful motivator and his enthusiasm was infectious. His vision was inspirational. We did not work to deadlines but to gentle nudges, and as one book followed another Steve became a great friend and part of our extended family. Sometimes when he came to visit, my son Mike would laughingly enquire, 'Steve, did you come to rattle the bucket?'

Over the years we worked our way from non-fiction to fiction and poetry and back to non-fiction. At first we had no book launches, and then they took place in Dublin and Cork until we found our way back home to Innishannon, and the launches took place in our local art gallery, The Private Collector, where the entire village gathered. I loved the at-home launches and Steve was always on for an Innishannon launch where we had singing, music and fun.

That last night on our way home from the final farewell

in Dingle, Lena, who had known Steve since she was a child, and I talked about his life and the gathering that had just taken place. She remarked that the general consensus of the people there was that Steve had enjoyed life. That, she decided, was how anyone would wish to be remembered.

Over the past two years I have worked on this book on bereavement which was to be published by Brandon, and just before his sudden death Steve had sent me his editorial notes which I was half-way through implementing when he died.

Epilogue

A Place Called Peace

You get used to being alone. At first every fibre of my being cried out in desolation at the loneliness, but gradually the spirit calms and strengthens. You quarry into your inner being. Our inner being is strong and deep. One of the spades to do this digging is creativity – our creativity is a pathway out of desolation into wholeness. Some of us see ourselves as not having a creative bone in our body but that is not so. We are a divine creation and I am convinced that in each one of us is a creative reservoir that sometimes goes untapped and in there is the healing well for many ills.

Some perceive creativity as being confined to the worlds of art, music and poetry, but creativity stretches across endless fields of human activities – cooking, wood turning, knitting, dressmaking, gardening, bee-keeping and countless other activities that engage our creative minds. These are the things that keep us human, rejuvenate us and renew our spirit.

Working with the earth was my greatest healer. During hours of digging, something calming and enriching seeps into the human spirit. It used to be one of life's mysteries, but a recent experiment in a New York university has discovered that working with the earth actually releases a certain soil bacterium that seeps into the body, removes confusion from the mind and increases stamina. It probably explains how our ancestors on the land survived poverty, hardship and famine. They were close to the earth and the animal world and both are sustaining.

I recently talked to a farmer whose young wife had died of cancer and he told me, 'The cows are comforting.' I could understand exactly what he meant. There is something solid and stable about cows. They spell out endurance and earthiness. Death exposes our fragility and vulnerability and there is no comfort in artificiality and shallowness. We need the sustenance of real people and solid routine until we have regained our equilibrium. We also need silence to soothe the mind and slowly absorb and come to terms with what has happened.

I found that visiting the grave helped and afterwards I would call into the nearby church and sit quietly for long periods. There is deep healing in the calming stillness of a quiet place. In bereavement the deep recesses of the mind need to be calmed and rested – sometimes a quiet body leads to a quiet mind.

Another coping tool I discovered is a grief journal. In the morning when a black cloud clung me to my bed, I tried writing. I didn't plan the writing, just let my pain flow onto the page. I kept a journal by the bed or under my pillow and used it early in the morning when the grief pain is deepest.

The act of writing
Eased my compressed pain
It poured off my pen
On to the open page.

Facing another day is a constant challenge. Simply dragging oneself out of bed is a huge effort. Straight into the shower first thing was a good start for me – not for cleansing but for stimulation! Having a shower sounds like a very mundane exercise, but it gets the blood in circulation and makes one feel like a member of the human race.

I tried to avoid the 'if only' or 'should have' cul-de-sac. That corner is strewn with regrets and the more we nurse them the bigger they get. One of them with which I struggled was the feeling that I should have been able to be more present to my loved ones in their final hours. Why did I not have the ability to be a greater comfort? Why did I not do *this*? Why did I not say *that*? The list was endless! But it was a futile exercise and if possible we should post a mental 'no entry' sign at that door!

Relaxation tapes helped me a lot when sleep refused to come or disappeared in the early hours. I accumulated a selection of tapes and CDs to ease the countless hours of tossing and turning. Walking helped as well. One of my friends told me 'walking releases the happy hormones.' She was right!

We should be good to ourselves in grief. In bereavement we are in intensive care, but we are both patient and nurse. Reflexology and massages, I found, kneaded out the knots of tension that are part of grieving. One of the most thoughtful gifts that I received when I was in a bad place was a lavender eye pillow. To lie down and put it over the eyes while listing to calming instrumental music soothes the soul – instrumental rather than vocal, as words can be intrusive.

A jug of fresh flowers on the kitchen table where our eye will constantly fall on them can be comforting too as colour affects our state of mind, so vibrant flowers can ease and nurture us.

Fresh Flowers

Give me a bunch
Of dew fresh flowers,
What if they will not last?
I cannot live in the future;
The present is all I ask.

A while back I took up meditation. When people hear of meditation they often think of enclosed orders and hermitages, but meditation has a place in the lives of ordinary Joe Soaps as well. It was part of a calmer lifestyle before the Celtic Tiger growled and ran us all into a stampede. Growing up in the country you spent a lot of time on your own, and meditation calms the turmoil of the mind in a similar way and leads to a more serene approach when facing the hurdles of life. Studies have shown that where a certain percentage of a population meditates, violent behaviour decreases. I found a book by John Maine that lays out the basic steps. Meditation, I discovered, is simple but not easy: Maine says that our minds are like trees full of chattering monkeys and in order to quieten them we need silence. Instead we often try shouting louder.

In the early days of grieving, the grief groove has to be ploughed and unfortunately we cannot run away from it. Grief has a long memory and like the snake in the grass can wait years to raise its remembering head. Maybe the grief that washed over England in the days following the death of Princess Diana was partly some of the suppressed grief for years of their own unmourned dead. Every nation has its own grief culture.

At the moment I am wondering about what we are doing to some of our funerals here in Ireland. Are we are turning them into reality TV? Funerals have turned into our biggest-attended church functions. Are they providing a connection point in our disconnected communities that have lost so many gathering points? This in itself is not a bad thing, but what about the bereaved? Do we need to have a look at what we are doing to the them? The bigger the tragedy, the bigger the crowds. Endless hours of hand-shaking, sometimes with people they do not even know, can turn into a mind-numbing exercise for traumatised people. Who can say slow down and think? Not the priest, because they are now almost afraid to open their mouths; not the undertaker, because he is providing a service; and certainly not the bereaved, who are too distraught to break the mould. It is preferable to the culture of pretending that death is 'nothing at all', but surely there must be a balance. Also the recent practice of taking large numbers of people to pubs and hotels after the funeral for a meal seems to me to be too much. This originated in the custom of taking people who had made a long journey back to the home for sustenance. But do big crowds comfort the bereaved? Also, at the time of a funeral nobody thinks of expense, but months afterwards bills have to be paid.

A few years ago I was at the funeral of a relative whose husband had died and as she was leaving the graveyard to go to a hotel as her children had arranged, she said plaintively, 'I just want to go back to my own house.' I said to her, 'Do exactly as you want to do', and she did. There is a lot of pressure on us to run with the herd, but there are times when we need to stop and work things out for ourselves.

Sometimes a project is good to focus the mind on something other than the all-consuming grief. While thus occupied, healing may happen and we could return to an easier place. Grieving is a Catch 22 situation! It saps our energy so we are unable to occupy ourselves with projects. Or we may go into a spin of activity as a distraction and exhaust ourselves.

Keeping Busy

Am I afraid to stop
In case all my pieces
Shatter apart?
Could I disintegrate
And never come back
Together again?

As we travel through grief we will work out what is best for us. Each person's grief journey is unique to them and we all cope in different ways.

After Con died in 2001 I wrote a book that I never had published but it served its purpose in that it took over my mind; I siphoned my grief into it. When Gabriel died in 2005 I redesigned the garden and the hours of digging kept me sane. The work was tough on the body but good for the mind. After Ellen died in 2009 I had the house re-roofed and insulated – while it was in progress I slept in the attic and every morning woke up to the sound of hammering on the roof, so I had to get up!

Looking back now I realise that these were all coping mechanisms. When in the grief groove we can go around endlessly in the same circle of desolation. A project helps to lift us out temporarily and prevents us getting stuck in the groove. When we return from the project the groove has healed a little and we may not sink down as deep.

On the first occasion when I met a sympathiser and did not cry I felt a great sense of relief. Strands of normality are reassuring. Going somewhere for the first time after a bereavement is a huge effort.

The Gap

We had gone
There together.
Now I go alone
And cannot
Fill the space;
Want to go home
Lock myself in
Where I do not
Have to hold back tears
And pretend to be normal.

Secrets

You are gone
So now I walk
The beach alone.
I pick up
A small round stone
Glistening with sea and sand,
Massage it through my fingers.
The smooth hard stone
Withholds the secrets
Of sea and land.

Enclosed and impenetrable,
It is as incomprehensible
As death.

It is difficult if we get dragged to unappealing places but if there is the slightest chance that something might help I tried to go. Coming home to an empty chair gets more bearable the oftener we do it.

In death we need ritual but in grief we all cope in different ways. We each find our own coping skills and we have within us deep reservoirs of unquarried strength. We will dig into these as we struggle on and be amazed at the veins of endurance that are buried in there.

Glen Waterfall

The roaring waterfall
Blew the crust
Off the hard wound of grief.
As pain burst forth
It screamed aloud
With the raging torrents.
But the determined water
Penetrated into the depths
Of locked up grief,

Showed no mercy.
I cried and screamed
With anger and relief
As foaming water
Washed out imprisoned pain.

When the storm abated
Icy water had cleansed
My inner being.
I was more at ease
With my deep sorrow.

Linked by Love

You are gone
And I am here
Wounded by your going,
Grieving for togetherness.
But we are more
Than we have shared.
Let not my staying
Or your going
Divide us now
Because you and I
Are closer than

Our earthly bodies.
Our love a rainbow
Bridging life and death
Links us now.

Welcome

A long wet winter
Drowns our spirit.
With souls sodden
From sheeting rain
We welcome in
The light of spring.
As birds released
From locked cages
To fly again.

Easter

Planted a lilac tree
Gift from a friend.
It rose from the earth
Like the risen Christ.
Friendship and resurrection,
Branches of the same tree.

Kindness

The warmth of your kindness
Kept me in my mind;
Its worth could not be measured,
It had goodness undefined;
You held out a caring hand
When I was full of pain;
You thawed my frozen being
And made me live again.

OTHER BOOKS BY
ALICE TAYLOR

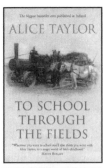

TO SCHOOL THROUGH THE FIELDS
Her classic account of growing up in the Irish
countryside, the biggest-selling book ever
published in Ireland.

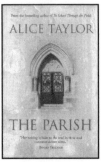

THE PARISH
In a series of vignettes of life in her village, Taylor
reasserts the priorities of public space and local
community, and explores the potential for a
future that achieves harmony between comfort
and the pressing need to respect the environment.

THE VILLAGE
The third of Taylor`s unique accounts of life
in the Irish countryside, and another massive
bestseller with universal appeal.

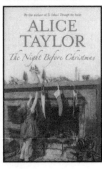

THE NIGHT BEFORE CHRISTMAS
A nostalgic, loving look back to a family firmly
rooted in tradition and humour and, in particular,
the Christmas traditions of her childhood.

QUENCH THE LAMP

A witty and lyrical memoir centring on the 1950s when the author and her friends were budding teenagers. Evokes the past vividly and without complaint as the years of hard labour were also filled with fun in a close-knit community.

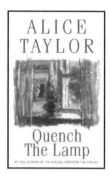

COUNTRY DAYS

Taylor takes her readers along the byways of Ireland and into the heart of the country. In stories by turn comic and poignant, she explores the character of family and friends, testing the bonds of concern and kindness which hold people together.

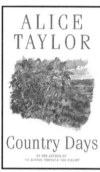

FICTION:

THE WOMAN OF THE HOUSE

A story of love for the home place and of the passions and jealousies it can inspire. Following his brutish father's unlamented death, young Danny Conway strives to rescue the family farm from ruin.

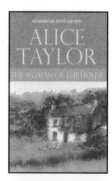

ACROSS THE RIVER

Taylor's second novel, a story of land, love and family set in rural Ireland. Sequel to *The Woman of the House*.

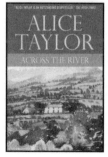

**FOR A COMPLETE LIST OF BOOKS
BY ALICE TAYLOR,
SEE WWW.OBRIEN.IE**